'50s & '60s Glass, Ceramics, & Enamel Wares

Designed & Signed

by Georges Briard, Sascha B.,
Bellaire, Higgins...

Leslie Piña

Georges Briard

Schiffer Publishing Ltd

77 Lower Valley Road, Atglen, PA 19310

for Jascha

Acknowledgments

Printed in Hong Kong
ISBN: 0-88740-935-0

Library of Congress Cataloging-in-Publication Data

Piña, Leslie A., 1947-
   '50s & '60s glass, ceramic, & enamel wares: designed & signed by George Briard, Sascha B., Bellaire, Higgins-/Leslie Piña.
      p.   cm.
   Includes bibliographical references and index.
   ISBN 0-88740-935-0
   1. Glassware–Collectors and collecting–United States–Catalogs.
  2. Glassware–United States–History–20th century–Catalogs.
  3. Pottery–Collectors and collecting–United States–Catalogs.
  4. Pottery–United States–History–20th century–Catalogs.
  5. Enameled ware–Collectors and collecting–United States–Catalogs.
  6. Enameled ware–United States–History–20th century–Catalogs. I. Title.
NK5112.P475 1996
738'.0973'09045–dc20   95-26284
                              CIP

Georges Briard and Philip Stetson made this book possible. Ralph and Terry Kovel helped me to find them. Thank you.

Others kindly provided information or lent objects to be photographed: Winslow Anderson, Cynthia Barta of Studio Moderne, Couroc, Lynn Davis, F. P. S. Archives, Elaine and Eli Friedman, Sylvia and Merv Glickman, Frances Higgins, Ralph and Terry Kovel, Ruth and Arthur Marcus, Donna McGrady, Paula and Steve Ockner (who not only provided us with many wonderful pieces to photograph for each chapter, but helped with the work), Elinor Polster, Suite Lorain Antiques, Donna and Rodney Wasserstrom, Dan Zusy and Michael Robertson, and Pfaltzgraff Pottery.

All Georges Briard vintage photographs, company catalogs, photographs of drinkware groupings and original artwork are courtesy of Jascha Brojdo (Georges Briard) and Philip Stetson. Thanks also to Jascha and Philip for proofreading Chapter One and to Paula Ockner for proofreading everything; any remaining errors are mine.

Of course, special thanks to Nancy and Peter Schiffer and the staff at Schiffer Publishing, and to Ramón, my partner with photography and life.

Preface

Memories of suburbia in the 1950s are colored by popular culture—black-and-white television, convertibles in colors that today's cars can only dream of, new fast foods, rock 'n roll, and modern design. Relatively few fashion-conscious consumers furnished these suburban homes with Herman Miller furniture, but many had an ashtray or set of tumblers with a Georges Briard signature. The fifties have been called (perhaps with tongue in cheek) the "golden age of design," and the Briard glassware and other items decorated with gold birds, gold fruit, and gold with colors brought a literal meaning to the phrase.

Whether caught in a bout of fifties nostalgia or because the designs still delight and intrigue, I recently began to notice and buy pieces with the Briard signature. Without actually collecting, something resembling a collection was being formed, which meant that it was time to go beyond visual amusement and learn something about the designer and company responsible for these objects. However, I had no success finding published information other than a line in an otherwise useful book that stated that Georges Briard was fictitious. Yet I had a paper tag with a small photograph of Georges Briard. The logical move was to ask the expert on antique and collectible trivia (among other things), Terry Kovel. "Is Georges Briard real?" I asked. "Let's find out," Terry replied, and she ran a line in *Kovels on Antiques and Collectibles* newsletter and in their syndicated newspaper column asking for information.

After letters arrived from around the country, Terry handed me the stack and smiled. One postcard had the name and phone number of a man presumed to be Georges Briard's partner. Did that mean that Georges Briard was real? It did, and the next thing I knew we were to meet for lunch in New York City (coincidentally, I had already planned a trip to research another designer). I arrived ten minutes early at a little restaurant near the United Nations building to find Art Deco wannabe decor, friendly service, tasty food, and Georges Briard toting a Louis Vuitton bag filled with vintage glass and catalogs. The rest is his story.

It is also a glimpse at the stories of some of the designers who were influenced by Briard and of others who independently contributed to a class of objects distinguished by a designer's signature on the front with the decoration. These remnants of the 1950s and 1960s accent today's homes as they did the modern interiors at mid-century. They are also attracting the attention of collectors smitten with fifties nostalgia and/or seeking modern design with a touch of camp. In an attempt to present this emerging collecting phenomenon, a definable category and style of decorative arts—designed and signed by—may also develop.

Contents

Georges Briard items in contemporary promotional photograph.

Introduction

According to glass historian Ada Polak, Emile Gallé was the first glass artist to put a full signature on the front of every piece of glass that he designed and produced at his factory. More than a piece of decorative art with a function, Gallé's art glass was meant to stand next to fine art—painting. Even if Gallé did not actually execute each piece, the signature would symbolize its high stature. Interestingly, the signature carried an additional reward—commercial success. Glass collectors, consumers if you will, enjoyed owning signed pieces, and Gallé, in turn, enjoyed signing them.

Other French glass artists began to realize the advantage in signing the front of their work, and by the late nineteenth century, the practice was widespread. When the flower of Art Nouveau wilted and its glass art became tired, the signature also faded from its prominent position on the work. It would not be used again commercially, to any extent, on decorative arts until after World War II when new attitudes about art, design, and utility entered the American home.

Although the designer's signature became common, if not expected, on many useful objects such as ceramics, relatively few designers placed their name on the front of the piece along with the decoration. One of the earliest and certainly the most commercial uses of this signature on the front was Georges Briard Designs with over twenty different companies manufacturing products that were made to be covered with his screened motifs and signature. "Designed and signed by Georges Briard" was a marketing motto that lent romance and desirability. These were, for the most part, ordinary objects. Yet, homemakers were not buying ordinary objects; they were buying a golden signature and a story.

Others designed and signed flat glass objects and tumblers with the Briard look at mid-century. Then in the late 1960s, graphic artist Peter Max began to incorporate a large signature into the design of posters plus a vast array of utilitarian objects. In some cases the signature was so large, it overpowered an already powerful graphic design.

The signature on the front was not always meant to enhance the commercial value. For example, when the Higginses did their most mass produced work at the Dearborn Glass Co. in the late 1950s, the gold decoration was also screened onto the glass pieces. Since engraving a signature onto the back was time-consuming, it too was screened. However, this gold signature required some drying time, and if it had been applied on the back of the piece, it would have stuck to a surface, so it was simply screened onto the front. For Sascha Brastoff and Marc Bellaire pottery, the signature on the front gave each piece a feeling of artistic originality.

There are certainly other signatures that were used on the front of mid-century decorative arts. Those shown in this book are among the most popular—both then and now.

Shallow bowl with Peter Max design printed on glass, produced by Houze Glass of Point Marion, Pennsylvania in the late 1960s. 9 1/2" diameter.

Scarf with Peter Max graphic and exaggerated signature, which becomes an important part of the overall design.

Value Guide

Many items shown here represent new collecting arenas. Not only are prices relatively erratic and inconsistent across regions of the country, in some instances, they are not established at all. In other words, many of these valuable decorative arts are not valued in places where they are not yet known or understood. The implications are exciting for the collector. As with every other collecting field, until word spreads, there will be less predictability and better hunting than with better known and more stable categories.

Because prices are subject to fluctuations even as this book goes to press, this guide can only provide a very general range. These values are based on asking and selling prices in the marketplace, excluding nonprofessional and often non-recurring markets, such as garage sales. Neither the author nor the publisher are responsible for any outcomes from consulting this guide. Life offers no guarantees. We do, however, wish you great fun and adventure in this playing field.

Price ranges (in U.S. dollars) appear at the end of captions in the order that the item was described in the caption excluding catalog pages. Position abbreviations such as L = left, TL = top left, etc. are used in captions. Prices are for items in perfect condition.

Chapter One
Georges Briard

"It costs no more to produce a good design than a bad one." *Georges Briard*

Georges Briard is an artist, a designer, and a businessman; he has also become something of a legend and an institution of postwar American popular culture. Born in the Russian Ukraine, Jascha Brojdo moved to Poland at the age of four. His father was a wealthy grain merchant who sold to European markets before the commodity was even planted. Never lacking material comforts, young Jascha enjoyed painting and sleeping late. Even as a teenager of fourteen or fifteen he had a reputation for his design sense and discerning taste. Whenever he traveled to Warsaw and other large cities, women would rely on his taste and give him orders for purchases such as handbags, hats, or household items. Jascha's judgment was never questioned; if he selected an item, it was right.

His parents never dreamt that he would leave such a perfect place, but Jascha wanted to visit his uncle, who was a doctor in Oak Park, Illinois. Knowing his son's habits well, his father warned Jascha that in America everyone began their day at 6:00 a.m. Not discouraged, Jascha agreed to practice waking up at 6:00 a.m. every morning for a month. His father even hired a maid to wake him.

Jascha arrived in Chicago in 1937 in the midst of the Depression—outfitted like a bride with his own linens, a fur coat, and everything any young man could need or not need. Just in case he forgot to bring something or might need anything new in this strange place, his parents sent him a monthly allowance of $3,000. Now in 1937 in Chicago, $3,000 could buy a house—and a nice one at that.

Ready to get an early start, he awoke at 6:00 a.m. the first morning, and the second, and then realized that even his uncle the doctor, who seemed to be the first one up, slept until 9:00 a.m. Things were already looking up.

1.1 Jascha Brojdo as an art student in Chicago.

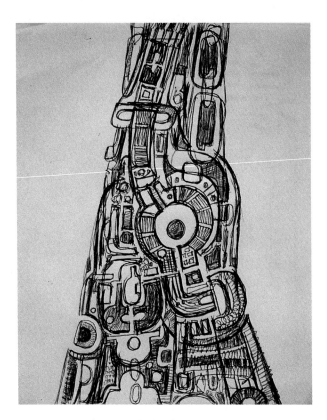

1.2 Doodle, blue ink on paper, 7 × 8 1/2".

1.4 Christmas phallus tree doodle, graphite pencil and red ink on paper, 8 1/2 × 11 1/2".

1.3 Abstract nude, graphite pencil on paper, 8 × 11 1/2".

1.5 Abstract face sketch, marker on paper, 19 × 24".

1.6 Faces sketch, marker on paper, 19 x 24".

1.7 Bird, marker on paper, 19 x 24".

The University of Chicago and the Art Institute of Chicago had a joint academic and art program which Jascha attended, and he eventually earned a Master of Fine Arts degree. At the street crossing by the Art Institute, at Michigan Avenue and Adams, there was a policeman who controlled traffic. In winter, however, Jascha had already stopped traffic as he paraded across the street in his fur coat. "Please, please wear another coat," pleaded the policeman. "I'll even buy it for you."

Not wanting to cause any further trouble, Jascha decided to buy a new coat. He went to Finchley's, a fine store where he spotted a nice gabardine and camel hair reversible coat that seemed understated enough. Without looking at the price tag, he glanced at the sales clerk and said, "I'll have it." The clerk looked at him as if he were mad, but he wrapped the coat while Jascha handed him $350.

While studying art, Jascha also learned about other aspects of American culture, and one of his early experiences concerned film. He recalled, "I was at the Art Institute and my English was very poor—I had been in the United States for maybe two months when someone told me that I should go to a movie audition being held at the Congress Hotel. It turned out that a movie company needed a Polish prince for a film they were going to make, so I went for the audition. Afterwards, the producer said that he was going to cast me for the part, but there was one thing wrong with me—my accent wasn't right. I looked at him sideways and said, 'what did you say?' After all, Polish was the only language I really knew well. Although I got the part as the prince and it went well, I decided then not to pursue a film career."

Things were going well in Chicago until one day word arrived from Poland that war had broken out in Europe. Mrs. Brojdo had been killed by a bomb; Mr. Brojdo had been sent to Siberia and died in a camp; and Jascha's thirteen-year-old sister had been sent to Siberia by the Russians, and she remained there until the end of the war. She now lives in California. Without a family, cut off from home and his allowance, Jascha went to the Art Institute to ask for a scholarship to complete his studies. "It wasn't just that I had been stupid enough to spend all my money and was penniless," he later explained, "but I really did deserve a scholarship." He was awarded a scholarship and studied painting and design.

During vacation he worked in the gift department at Marshall Field department store. One day a woman came in to buy a gift and asked for assistance.

"I will be delighted to help you," volunteered Jascha.

"This is not right...that is not right...I am looking for a gift... something very special," complained the customer.

"There is one very special item...something unique, but it is rather expensive," he tempted.

"Yes, yes, do show it to me," she responded, just as Jascha had predicted.

An old clock was sitting on a shelf—a fixture. It had been there for years just telling time but was otherwise ignored. Jascha hadn't the faintest idea what to charge for this instant treasure, so he excused himself to inquire about the packing. "How much can I charge for this monstrosity?" he discreetly asked the store manager. After he was supplied with an arbitrary and appropriately outrageous price,

1.8 Abstract painting.

he returned to the customer. "Madam, it is beautiful, but I am afraid that it is too expensive for anybody," he toyed.

"Pack it," she said.

In 1938 when a twenty-dollar sale was considered big, the sale of a store fixture for hundreds made young Jascha a hero. He was given a tea party at the store. Two weeks later, a young woman came in carrying the clock. "They did it to her again," she explained, as her mother's money was refunded and the clock was returned to the shelf.

Jascha would have other opportunities at heroism during the war, but he had already learned how fleeting the pleasures can be. After graduating from art school in 1942 he joined the United States Army. Curiously, he was appointed to teach English, a language he had just barely learned himself, to illiterate recruits. One day the captain called him into his office.

"I've done some checking up on you Brojdo. I would like to know how someone with your education and background can speak the way you do?"

"Do you mean my English is bad?"

"Your English is fine, but why must you end every sentence with F#@* and *%#! and F!@#?"

"I am only trying to sound just like everyone else," Jascha assured.

"Oh my God!" exclaimed the captain, realizing that Jascha hadn't the faintest idea what the words meant. From then on, Jascha was careful to look up the meanings of all new words before he used them.

Obviously fluent in Russian, he was assigned to Army Intelligence as a Russian interpreter. Assuming that he had natural language ability, the Army then sent him to Harvard to study geo-politics and German. After graduating from the program with German lan-

guage fluency, he was called to Washington. Not knowing quite what to expect, he went with his wife Bronya, whom he had married in Cambridge, Massachusetts. "Some idiot heard a tape of me speaking and decided that I could pass for a German," Jascha explained, "when in fact I spoke with a perfect Russian-Polish-American accent. They wanted to drop me behind enemy lines so that I could impersonate a German. Listen, I told them, if I ever decide to commit suicide, I will pick my own way and my own time. I would be crazy to let you drop me even behind American lines." So Jascha was sent to Europe as a Russian interpreter. He spent eighteen months in a luxurious office in a magnificent part of the Alps doing absolutely nothing. Nothing useful, that is, until after the war when he participated in every champagne party that the Americans gave for the Russians. Being in the Third Army, he served as a Russian interpreter for General Patton's staff.

Just as he had been taught to come prepared when he first arrived in the United States from Poland, Jascha remembered to pack well when he was sent to Europe for the war. As he sat on the bed in the barracks and began to unpack, he noticed some officers watching him.

"He has them!" exclaimed one of the officers.

"Has what?" asked Jascha.

"Shoelaces!"

"Shoelaces?"

"Yes. Will you sell us some of your shoelaces?" asked the officer. As if it was not enough that they were in the middle of a world war, there had to be a shortage of shoelaces.

"I would be happy to give you my shoelaces," Jascha offered. "You don't have to buy them."

It turned out well. Jascha had six pairs of laces. For three pairs, he got a Leica camera (since the officers evidently had more than six

1.9 Table setting, oil on canvas, 30 x 39" without frame.

1.10 Abstract faces, 13 1/2 x 17" without frame.

Leica cameras). Later, he went to Zwemmer's in London and traded the camera and a silver cigarette case for a book of Picasso lithographs. So one could say that he traded shoelaces for Picassos.

Being stationed in Germany all those months with nothing to do was tiring, so Jascha managed to obtain passes for frequent trips to Paris. Jascha had a good friend by the name of Charles Bolles Rogers, who headed the Red Cross in Europe and was headquartered at Claridges Hotel in London. Rogers was very wealthy and influential. One day, during Jascha's leave in London, Rogers gave him a letter of introduction to deliver to another friend. The friend was Gertrude Stein, who lived in Paris. Without any telephones to phone ahead, on Jascha's next trip to Paris he went to call on Ms. Stein. It was afternoon when he arrived at her home, excited and also concerned. His heart was pounding rather fast, something unfamiliar to him. He approached the building, gained his composure, and then knocked. A woman opened the door.

"May I see Gertrude Stein?"

"I am Gertrude Stein, but who are you?"

"I am Jascha Brojdo, and I have a letter for you."

He was ushered into a beautiful apartment filled with wonderful paintings. After a pleasant visit, he asked Gertrude's friend Alice B. Toklas if there was anything he could do for them. "Yes," she replied in fun, "we need Hershey bars more than anything."

Before his next visit to Paris, Jascha managed to amass thirty-six jumbo chocolate bars (some even with nuts). His army buddies called him a "man with a mission," the mission being to collect chocolate bars for Gertrude Stein and Alice B. Toklas.

When Jascha returned to Paris and delivered the chocolate, Alice turned to Gertrude and said, "thank you for this gift is just not enough," and suggested that they do something special for Jascha. They decided to speak to a good friend of Gertrude's, David Kahnweiler, who happened to be the exclusive agent for Pablo Picasso.

Shortly after returning to Germany and still a stand-by Russian interpreter for Army Intelligence, Jascha received a call from Paris. A man introduced himself as David Kahnweiler and invited Jascha to meet him at the famous bar in the Ritz hotel. Jascha got an army pass and arrived in Paris one week later. After a drink at the bar, Kahnweiler took him to a garage behind the hotel. When the door was opened, the garage was so packed with Picassos that the paintings practically fell out. Kahnweiler pulled out a very large canvas and offered Jascha seventeen of the same size for $50,000. It didn't take a rocket scientist to calculate what they were worth, even wholesale in the early 1940s. Unfortunately, it never occurred to Jascha that he could have purchased one or two of the paintings instead of the entire group. Ten years later, he and Bronya traveled to Paris in style, and visited Kahnweiler in his very elegant gallery. "I tried so hard to make you rich," he complained, "but you just wouldn't let me."

In 1947 Jascha was discharged from the Army and went to New York to work for Max Wille selling decorative items. Wille was one of those rare individuals—a genuinely nice person with excellent taste. They had met while Jascha was still at art school, and Wille had sold some of Jascha's hand-decorated toleware. This time, Jascha would be selling Wille's lines. He began working in sales, and then around

1950, his design career took off. Jascha brought blank trays along on a trip to Vinalhaven Island off the coast of Maine. The island was named for the Vinal family, and poet Harold Vinal was a friend of Jascha's. During the visit, Jascha painted the trays and then carried them back to New York for Wille to sell. "They were a fantastic success," he recalled. "Every woman who had a little shop wanted them."

The toleware that he designed and sold as a student was signed "Brojdo" on the back. In those days designers did not ordinarily lend their names to commercial products; if they did, the name was on the back of the item along with the company logo. Since the new commercial adventure was not necessarily part of Jascha's artistic goals, he approached Wille. "Max," he said, "I think these should be sold under a designer pseudonym—I want to save my name for more important work."

Max and his wife had recently lost their pet dog. While at a dog show, they were both captivated by a beautiful briard, so Max asked Jascha, "how about Briard? We'll call you Briard and use the first name Georges with an 's' at the end to make it very French."

In that business, product lines were usually good for one season of about three to six months. They did not expect the Georges Briard name and signature to last any longer than the trays on which

1.11 Abstract faces, 12 x 17 3/4" without frame.

1.12 Metal tray in dark green with "Heaven Can Wait" motif, 25 3/4" length.

1.13 Metal tray in black with coats of arms, 25 3/4" length.

14

it was signed, but Max and Jascha had become partners and were full of ideas for more commercial lines. "Georges Briard" would have to stay, and Jascha would continue to save his real name for his paintings. While close friends and family continued to call him Jascha, the name Georges Briard became associated with the man as well as the product signature; from then on the public would know him as Mr. Briard.

One of their ideas was to use gold—22 karat gold—to decorate glass. This gold decoration needed to be printed or screened on, so bent flat glass seemed to be the logical solution. The Bent Glass Co. made bent flat glass lighting fixtures for ceilings. In order to accommodate Briard's more artistic ideas, they formed Glass Guild to manufacture and market the new product. Two types of glass were used: "aura crystal" was a colorless textured glass, and "white opal" was an

opaque white glass that provided an extraordinary surface to show off the gold and black screened patterns. The bent white opal often varied in thickness and had slightly irregular corners, giving it a handmade quality and additional charm. Glass Guild was so successful—Georges Briard Designs was so successful—that it quickly became the biggest factor in the Bent Glass factory.

Many years later Jascha went on a house tour on Sutton Place—one of those events where homeowners open their homes to the public in order to raise money for a good cause. As he entered an apartment with a huge foyer, he could not believe what he saw. Every wall of the foyer was covered with Glass Guild serving pieces. Jascha was speechless (but not for long). "Isn't this a little too much?" he asked.

1.14 Early wood tray with plant on gold, 28 3/4" length.

1.15 Early round wood tray with bird motif, signed "Brojdo" on the back, 17" diameter.

1.16 Early round wood tray, signed "Brojdo" on the back, 10 1/2" diameter; with 4" wood box.

The lady of the house looked at him somewhat surprised and said proudly, "These are all by Georges Briard!"

As long as the Briard decorations were so successful on the bent glass, it was decided that they ought to be used on other surfaces as well. Undecorated pieces made by major glass companies such as Libbey, and especially Anchor Hocking, were the answer. Serving pieces could be decorated, added to, reassembled, and resold. An undecorated item that normally sold at Woolworth's could be decorated and carried at Bloomingdale's. Glass was by no means the only suitable material. For example, Columbian Enamel distributed plain enameled steel cookware to five-and-dime stores. This inexpensive whiteware, once made by many companies, was a dying industry; only a few, like Columbian, remained. Briard got the bright idea to decorate these with colorful "Green Garden," or "Coq D'or" or "Ambrosia" (pineapple) patterns. He also added brass-plated warming stands and used color, in addition to white, enamel backgrounds. It was all very romantic. The company's success could be attributed to their ability to capitalize on this romanticism and to see things that others did not see. They also realized that they could do things that other manufacturers could not do by themselves. Briard could invent a design and send it off to another company to fabricate the item. Georges Briard Designs would then sell it to a retailer, while the other company would do the shipping. Or, Georges Briard Designs would take parts—a cheese board, a little knife, a chain, a pottery dip cup—and assemble them in an innovative way. They would then distribute a new and complete product. It was the right idea at the right time, in the 1950s.

Collaboration with many different compa-

nies without complicating the relationship with ownership was the key to Briard's diversification. Among the most successful of these symbiotic relationships were those with Glass Guild in Jamaica, New York and with Woodland in Glen Falls, New York. Woodland made high quality wood products, and their walnut or oak cheese boards could readily accommodate Briard's raised gold designs on enameled metal tiles or an occasional Italian ceramic tile insert. Woodland made the product and paid Briard a royalty for the design. Briard made a prototype for each one, directed and supervised its execution, and checked the result for quality. Georges Briard Designs was also paid a sales commission for marketing and distribution. It became a tremendous business, especially in the 1960s.

Always open to the possibility of new markets and new products, Briard found some diversions in ceramics in the early 1960s. Hyalyn Porcelain in Hickory, North Carolina commissioned him to design modern shapes for a line of bisque porcelain produced in white and a limited number of earthtone colors. Pleasantly simple forms accommodated Briard stylized motifs; wonderful raised gold abstractions against the smooth ceramic surface had the spirit of Wilhelm Kåge's Art Deco silver patterns on Gustavsberg pottery from Sweden. Briard called the series "Midas."

A woman by the name of Esta Huttner owned the Peerless Art Co. in Brooklyn, New York. Her specialty was a very well-executed raised gold decoration on glass, which she made for some Briard glassware. With her expertise, Hyalyn was able to incorporate the raised gold onto their porcelain. The style and the material was particularly appropriate for lamps, so Lightolier of Secaucus, New Jersey used Briard Hyalyn porcelain vases for a line of lamp bases.

1.17 Georges Briard.

Where the Hyalyn designs epitomized Briard's sophisticated yet whimsical abstractions and no holding back on gold, the Pfaltzgraff Pottery venture was totally atypical. A family-owned and managed company in York, Pennsylvania since its founding in 1811, Pfaltzgraff remains today the leading and the oldest American manufacturer of dinnerware. Briard designed a tablesetting of traditional-looking octagonally-shaped stoneware in earthy brown and green. Introduced in the early 1960s, the pattern was called "Heritage." After about ten months, and thinking that the pattern was a flop, Pfaltzgraff offered Briard an apology and a generous payment to break the original contract. If he accepted the check, it would have meant that he was well paid for the design but would no longer receive royalties. Briard chose not to accept the check, and Pfaltzgraff decided to keep the pattern in production. Briard, not wishing to be associated with products sold to mass merchandisers, requested that they omit the "Designed by Georges Briard" imprinted on the bottom of any subsequent production, which they did. More than thirty years later, Heritage is still a best seller with royalties sent to Briard all those years.

1.19 Pfaltzgraff Heritage pattern, current. Photo courtesy Pfaltzgraff Pottery.

1.18 Pfaltzgraff Heritage pattern, early 1960s.

Briard had started with the premise that the commercial ventures were somehow in a separate and different dimension from fine art. They were business; Jascha Brojdo was an artist. His genius was the ability to smoothly blend his art with business. Intrigued by the difference between good and bad design on both aesthetic and practical grounds, he believed that he could produce a good design for the same money, if not less, than a bad design. He went on to prove again and again that good design was good business.

In love with Modern Art, Briard had been first introduced in Chicago, where the school was housed in the same building as the museum galleries displaying modern European avant-garde art. Briard's paintings were unquestionably modern, and he used modern concepts in his best commercial work. He was also very versatile, and at the same time he was quoted as saying, "We must always try to preserve the link with the emotionally gratifying past" (Reese). It is not surprising that elements of historic style can be found incorporated into many of his designs, even modern ones.

Although he considered himself a painter first, Briard's career had been spent working more as an industrial designer with materials such as glass, enameled metal, wood, ceramics, textiles, and paper. He had not, however, tried working with plastics, which were considered to be more suited to industrial and commercial applications. Plastic dinnerware, melamine, became the next vehicle for Briard's patterns, which ranged from modern to traditional. On December 9, 1965, Allied Chemical introduced Artisan melamine dinnerware in sixteen patterns by Georges Briard to seventy home furnishings editors representing fifty newspapers, trade periodicals, and syndicated columns including *New York Times, New York Herald Tribune, Chicago Tribune, Home Furnishings Daily, American Home, and Better Homes and Gardens.* In 1964 Esta Huttner had introduced Briard to Philip Stetson of Stetson China, and he did some consulting work for Stetson. At that time, Allied Chemical purchased the old New York Times building and converted it to consumer products. They also purchased Stetson Products, which made melamine and already had a relationship with Briard. Phil Stetson continued to run Stetson Products for Allied until 1968, when he left to purchase retiring Max Wille's interest in Georges Briard Designs.

Because plastics had been associated with industry rather than art, Briard helped to blur the boundary between the two. "No one needs to make apologies for plastics," assured Briard in a 1965 interview for *Home Furnishings Daily*. "The plastic revolution is not only here to stay, it has already greatly altered the world." Plastic was undeniably convenient, efficient, and economical, but it had not yet been seriously considered as a vehicle for personal expression. Once again, Briard was about to make the ordinary a bit extraordinary, as he had already done with enameled whiteware and the plainest of glass. He explained: "Too often, a designer is basically someone who sits there in a corner thinking up designs and drawing pictures. However, I am more philosophically an industrial designer, concerned with design, but also with product, and price, and market. First, the product must be desirable and aesthetically pleasing—there is no room to compromise when it concerns good design. Next, it has to retail at a certain price range. When I was designing an item, I was partially motivated by a particular range of prices. And Anchor Hocking, God bless its soul, was made for me, because the dishes that you call—you know, the ordinary dishes—gave me a chance to get into the right price range. They may have been cheap, but I could still make them glamorous. I could take an ordinary plate, apply a gold design, drill a hole, attach a knife on a chain, then say, 'here.' It not only took a pretty picture; it took knowledge of the item—and that women wanted to serve the dip with potato chips around it."

When in 1965 Briard designed sixteen patterns for Stetson's Allied melamine, for a moment, plastic dishes became glamorous. Jascha and Bronya even tried them for formal dining: they set the table with melamine plates with his Poppy pattern, a centerpiece of live poppies, fine silver and crystal, and they served an elegant dinner. The guests never knew they were eating on plastic.

Promotional material used words like "bold, sophisticated, high style, distinctive." A 45-piece service for eight retailed for $29.95 and $39.95. Briard was keenly aware of the homemaker's struggle to retain identity and individuality and to resist standardization. He promised "to give them bread, but gave them roses."

And roses were returned to him. In 1966 the National Housewares Manufacturers Association (NHMA) started a Design in Housewares Award Program. Among the 94 products selected from 61 manufacturers was Allied Chemical's Artisan line. Four of Briard's patterns—Wheatland, Eden, Blue Sonata, and White Sonata—were chosen by a board of five leading industrial designers: Gene Bordinat of Ford Motor Co., Jon W. Hauser of Jon W. Hauser Inc., Tucker P. Madawick of RCA, Arthur J. Pulos from Syracuse University, and Harold Zierhut of Zierhut-Vedder-Shimano Design.

By the time Stetson and Briard put together the Allied Chemical project, the times were already changing. The Sixties revolutions—political, social, cultural—were at hand and could be heard in song lyrics and music that became louder and louder as the decade progressed. The Ozzie and Harriet Nelson and Beaver Cleaver family images were fading. Suburban women were becoming less enthusiastic about staying at home playing hostess in shirtwaist dresses or peddlepusher pants, entertaining husbands' bosses, or serving chips and dips and drinks to regular card game friends.

Cultural change impacted merchandising. Where large department stores with once endless floor space had displayed twenty or thirty stock keeping units (SKUs) of a Briard pattern—bar glasses, snack bowls, cheese boards, serving trays, warming buffets, and every other imaginable little hostess necessity that Briard had dreamt up—they later carried only three or five. The decade from the mid 1950s to the mid 1960s may or may not have been golden, but it was clearly over. If cultural change had altered the American market, then Georges Briard Designs needed to follow this change in order to stay ahead.

Stetson's new partnership brought restructuring. Georges Briard Designs bid farewell to Glass Guild and Woodland. Although Briard continued to introduce hundreds of new barware patterns and a successful china dinnerware series called "Private Collection," their biggest product line from 1969 until 1989 was bar serving accessories, including ice buckets. From generic vinyl to outrageous plastic-lacquer "Memphasis" models, Georges Briard Designs had the distinction of being the largest maker and seller of ice buckets in the world. The new market understandably included commercial customers, especially hotel chains.

As the marketplace changed, more products were made overseas in places like Thailand, the Philippines, Taiwan, and Japan. It was not without irony that Georges Briard Designs ultimately sent designs to Japan to be manufactured. Not long after the war ended, the Japanese government had decided to try to improve their image. Dissatisfied with their reputation for exporting cheap and unoriginal goods, they wished to make and export higher quality products. Without any specific plan, they sent one of their leading architects, Junzo Yoshimura, to the United States to select a consultant designer. Briard was riding the crest of his popularity; he and his wife were brought to Japan, where they spent six fascinating weeks being flown from city to city in a private plane, chauffeured about the Japanese landscape, and waited on as if they were royalty.

Some years later, Briard was in the giftware department of B. Altman & Co., and he could not believe his eyes. Right next to a beautiful display of signed Briards was a display of knockoffs made in, yes, Japan. He called in the buyer and shouted, "Mike! What are you doing? Have you lost your mind?"

"Stop, stop, don't get excited," said the buyer. "I did it on purpose, and I'll prove something to you." If the Briard item was selling for ten dollars, the Japanese copy was about three-fifty. The buyer promised that at the end of the day the unsigned copies would be left. And they were.

Items by Georges Briard Designs may have been priced higher than the copies, but they were still priced right. Their desirability could be attributed partly to the fact that they were affordable, but mostly because they were designed well. Once the consumer had been touched by the Briard mystique, there was little left for the competition.

Today, women who were married in the 1950s remember vividly how thrilling it was to receive gifts signed by Georges Briard. Tired of seeing "violets" on everything from tableware to shelf pieces, Briard designs were like a breath of fresh air. They were totally in touch with the times and what the public wanted. First, the designs were new and very appealing; second, the lavish, yet tasteful, use of gold lent an air of opulence and glamour even to ordinary pieces; third, and perhaps the most extraordinary feature, was the signature. On the front of every item and incorporated right into the design, Briard boldly displayed his name. "Designed and signed by Georges Briard" was more than a marketing motto; it was magic. Even though millions of items were produced with this signature, each one could be individually admired and desired.

The most mundane of cookware was transformed into a product of quality by the addition of a Georges Briard motif and generous application of 22-karat gold in the design, on handles, and on rims. The design, the gold, the signature, the pricing, and the timing were ingredients for an awesome merchandising event. Perhaps more wedding and shower gifts bore the Briard signature than any other giftware category in mid-century America.

Briard continued to come up with innovations for new giftware niches. For example, he created a line of gift-boxed products that enabled the shopper to purchase a complete moderately-priced gift in one package. One of the most popular of these was a bathroom set comprised of two glasses and two small linen towels, each complete with poodle motif and a Georges Briard signature. Even the packaging was thoughtfully decorated. Retailing for five dollars, the set was the perfect wedding shower gift, and it sold by the thousands. Another item was a simple oil and vinegar cruet set made by Anchor Hocking. With the addition of gold speckles, a gold-plated chain, and the letters "V" for vinegar and "O" for oil, it was packaged in another Briard gift box. Also retailing for five dollars, the perfect hostess gift had been created, and it sold equally well.

1.20 Department store display of Georges Briard products and original paintings.

1.21 Georges Briard display at Stix, Baer & Fuller in St. Louis, Missouri.

1.22 Store display.

1.23 Lazarus department store display with sign: "The signature of Georges Briard...means new provocative fashions in bent glass serving pieces that lend that extra touch to snacks or important dinner serving."

The proverbial whole was definitely more than the sum of its parts, especially according to Briard. Never enough to just decorate existing items, he invented new ones by cleverly combining components. Tile inserts on cheese boards, small dip bowls suspended over large chip bowls, and boxed gift sets were market novelties. Lines of hostess and bar accessories with coordinating design and signature made Briard items instant collectibles, evidenced by the fifties' brides who saved these little treasures long after they and other gifts and purchases had gone their separate ways.

1.24 Georges Briard with Silver Damask serving bowl.

1.25 Georges Briard with Silver Damask glasses.

Certainly other companies had products that were also priced well and even designed well at mid-century. Briard, however, offered more than a product; he offered a cultural phenomenon that included art, fashion, merchandising, gift-giving, entertaining, interior decoration, and perhaps the most fascinating of all—collecting. "Designed and signed by Georges Briard" was magical at mid-century. The magic is still there for collectors, and, for some, includes an added bonus of nostalgia.

1.27 Georges Briard and Philip Stetson standing in front of a Briard painting in his Manhattan apartment in 1995.

Below:
1.26 Original drawing by Georges Briard.

1.28 Front cover of Oct. 1, 1957 Price List.

1.30 Glass Guild items in May 1, 1958 Price List.

1.29 Glass Guild's Seascape in Oct. 1, 1957 Price List.

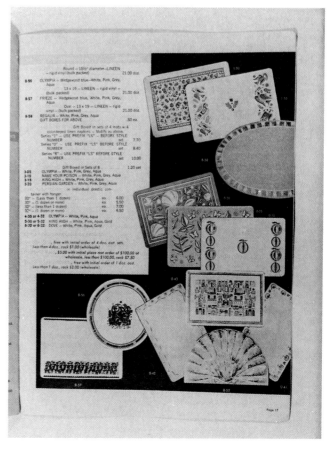

1.31 Page from Oct. 1, 1958 Price List.

22

1.32 Mosaic Art by Glass Guild in Oct. 1, 1959 Price List.

1.33 Glass Guild formed glass accessories in Oct 1, 1959 Price List.

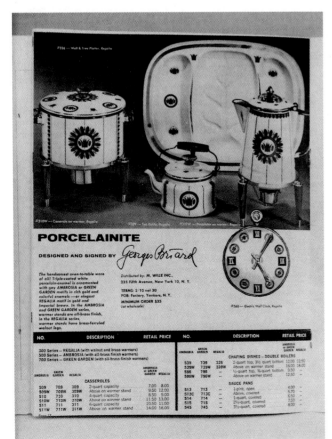

1.34 Porcelainite in Oct. 1, 1959 Price List.

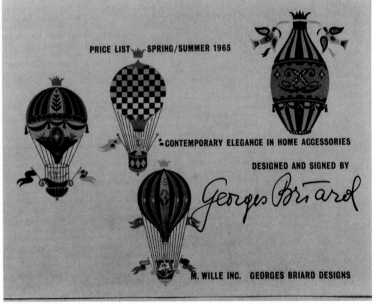

1.35 Cover of Spring/Summer 1965 Price List.

23

1.36 Cover photo for 1961-62 catalog.

1.38 Town & Country pattern.

1.37 Back cover of 1961-62 catalog.

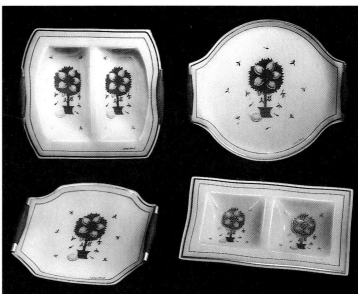

1.39 Lemon Tree pattern.

24

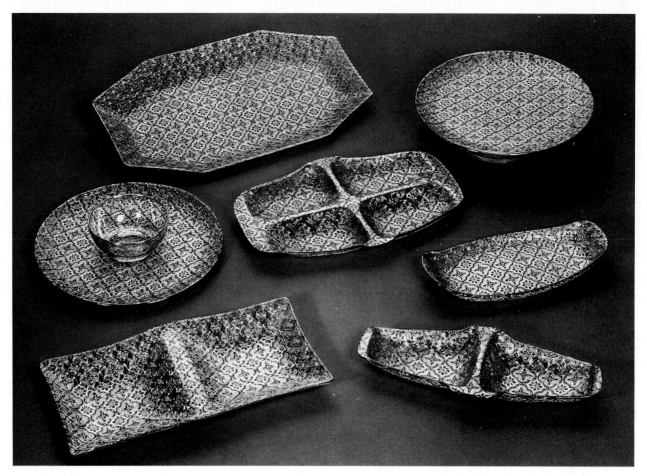

Above:
1.40 Iberian bent glass servers: top left, oblong hexagon 10 x 18"; top right, cake stand 11"; right center, dip server 14"; center, 4-section contour 9 1/2 x 14"; left center, contour relish; bottom left, 2-section server 8 x 14"; bottom right, 2-section contour 5 1/2 x 13 1/2".

Below:
1.41 Iberia.

1.42 Fancy Free.

1.43 Fancy Free.

1.44 Carrara.

1.45 Fleur Noir.

1.46 Sunflower.

1.47 Op Art.

1.48 Inside back cover of Sept. 1, 1960 Price List. Clockwise from top: Persian Garden, Regalia, Paradise, Heritance, Facade, Ambrosia, Embassy; center - Sonata.

1.49 East Wind from 1958 Price List.

1.50 Page from 1958 Price List.

"SUNFLOWER" Bent-Glass Accessories by GLASS GUILD
#9819 Hexagon Tray, 10 x 18"
#9886W Serving Tray, 10 x 12" #9809 Two-Section Server, 13 x 15" #9818 Hexagon, 11"
#9811 Two-Section Server, 8 x 14"

1.51 Sunflower bent glass accessories by Glass Guild: TL serving tray with wood handles; BL 8 x 14" 2-section server; C 13 x 15" 2-section server; TR 10 x 18" 8-sided tray; BR 11" hexagon tray.

1.52 Sunflower bent glass accessories by Glass Guild: TL round tray; BL serving tray with wood handle; TC square tray; C 2-section tray; BC small hexagon; TR hexagon with gold border; BR square with gold border.

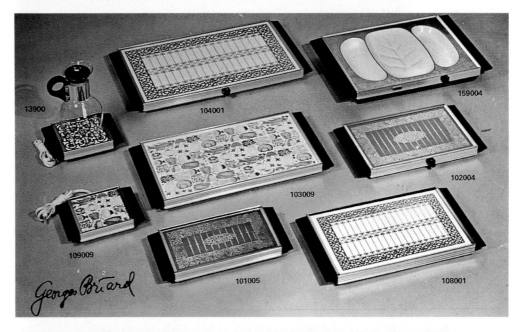

1.53 Hot Butlers: TL 6" square Spanish Gold with carafe; BL 6" square Melange; TC 13 x 22" Spanish Gold; C 11 x 19 1/2" Melange; BC 6 x 12" Town & Country Gold; TR Well-in-Tree with Town & Country; CR 7 x 12" Town & Country Silver; BR 10 x 16" Spanish Gold.

1.54 Town & Country Gold: TL Hot Butler; BL 12 1/4 x 15" 2-dip with 6" tile; TR 11 x 12 1/2" 1-dip with 4" tile; BR 7 x 13 1/2" oblong tray with 4" tile.

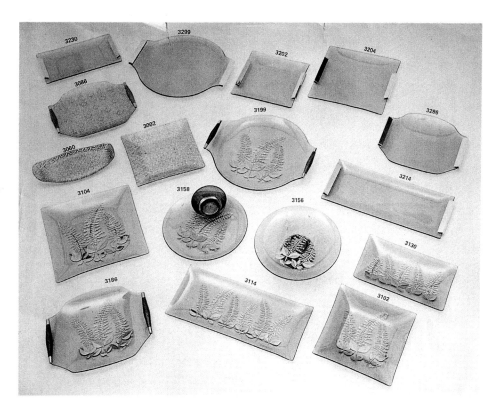

1.55 Plates and trays with Iberia, Fern on Smoke, and Smoke with chrome handles.

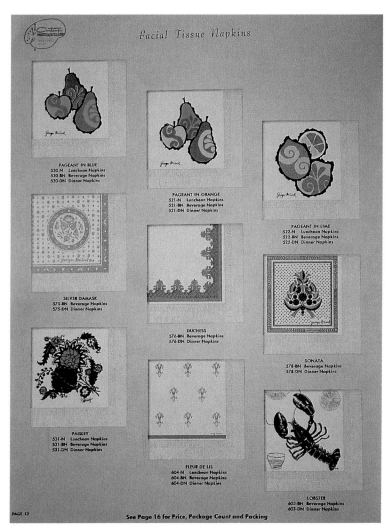

1.56 Georges Briard items in 1964 Contempo Paperware catalog, by Beach Products Inc: top row, Pageant in Blue, Orange, and Lime; RC Silver Damask; LC Sonata.

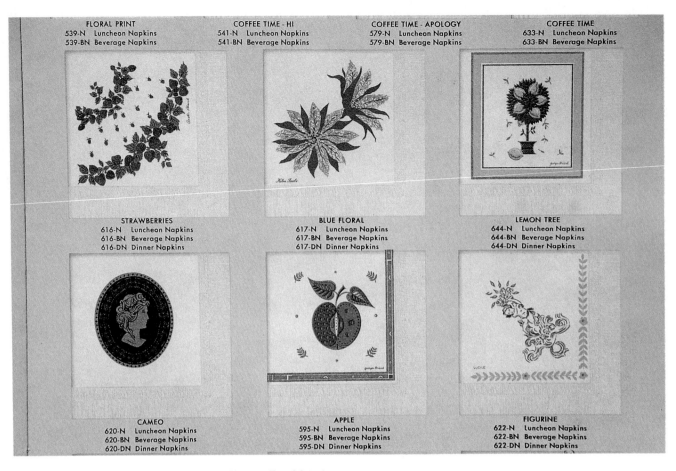

FLORAL PRINT		COFFEE TIME - HI		COFFEE TIME - APOLOGY		COFFEE TIME	
539-N	Luncheon Napkins	541-N	Luncheon Napkins	579-N	Luncheon Napkins	633-N	Luncheon Napkins
539-BN	Beverage Napkins	541-BN	Beverage Napkins	579-BN	Beverage Napkins	633-BN	Beverage Napkins

STRAWBERRIES		BLUE FLORAL		LEMON TREE	
616-N	Luncheon Napkins	617-N	Luncheon Napkins	644-N	Luncheon Napkins
616-BN	Beverage Napkins	617-BN	Beverage Napkins	644-BN	Beverage Napkins
616-DN	Dinner Napkins	617-DN	Dinner Napkins	644-DN	Dinner Napkins

CAMEO		APPLE		FIGURINE	
620-N	Luncheon Napkins	595-N	Luncheon Napkins	622-N	Luncheon Napkins
620-BN	Beverage Napkins	595-BN	Beverage Napkins	622-BN	Beverage Napkins
620-DN	Dinner Napkins	595-DN	Dinner Napkins	622-DN	Dinner Napkins

1.57 Georges Briard items in 1964 Contempo catalog: TR Lemon Tree; BC Apple.

1.58 Persian Garden paper table cover, napkins, cups, and plates in 1964 Contempo catalog.

Matched Ensembles

PERSIAN ENSEMBLE

615-N	Luncheon Napkins
615-BN	Beverage Napkins
615-DN	Dinner Napkins
615-BT	Table Cover
615-HC	9 oz. Plastic Lined Hot Cups
615-P7	7" Round Plates
615-P9	9" Round Plates

1.59 Artisan melamine dinnerware from Allied Chemical Corp. in seven patterns by Georges Briard.

1.60 Artisan melamine dinnerware, mid 1960s: TL Sunflower with Russet Brown cup; BL Bombay with Cocoa Brown cup; TR Duchess Green with Granada Green cup; BR Spanish Gold with Antique Gold cup.

1.61 Très Briard ceramic ashtrays with molded relief designs: TL 8 1/2" round Chrysanthemum; CL 7 3/4" square Lion; BL 6 1/4 x 7 1/2" Owl; TC 8 1/2" square Sunburst; BC 8 1/2" round Blue Flower; TR 6 1/2 x 9 1/4" Royal Chess; CR 5 1/4 x 9 1/2" Social Lion; BR 8 1/4" round Painted Daisy. 20-40 each

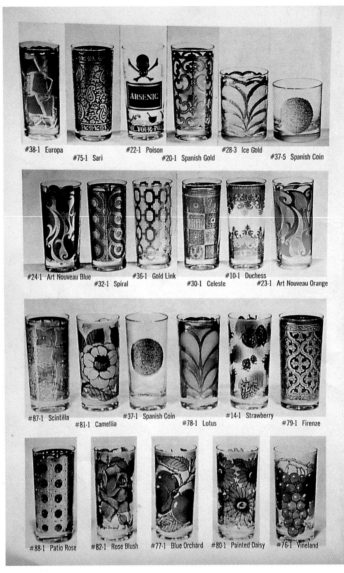

1.62 Glassware from Spring/Summer 1966 Price List. Top row: #38-1 Europa, #75-1 Sari, #22-1 Poison, #20-1 Spanish Gold, #28-3 Ice Gold, #37-5 Spanish Coin; second row: #24-1 Art Nouveau Blue, #32-1 Spiral, #36-1 Gold Link, #30-1 Celeste, #10-1 Duchess, #23-1 Art Nouveau Orange; third row: #87-1 Scintilla, #81-1 Camellia, #37-1 Spanish Coin, #78-1 Lotus, #14-1 Strawberry, #79-1 Firenze; bottom row: #88-1 Patio Rose, #82-1 Rose Blush, #77-1 Blue Orchard, #80-1 Painted Daisy, #76-1 Vineland.

Left:
1.62 Glassware from Spring/Summer 1966 Price List. Top row: Europa, Sari, Poison, Spanish Gold, Lotus, Spanish Coin; second row: Art Nouveau Blue, Spiral, Gold Link, Celeste, Duchess, Art Nouveau Orange; third row: Scintilla, Camellia, Spanish Coin, Lotus, Strawberry, Firenze; bottom row: Patio Rose, Rose Blush, Blue Orchard, Painted Daisy, Vineland. 4-8 each

Below:
1.63 L'Oignon ironstone serving accessories: bake 'n serve casseroles, canister sets, coffee and demitasse services, mugs, jam 'n jelly dishes, chip 'n dips, cheese boards.

1.64 Melange ice bucket, tumbler, and serving pieces in baked enamel on metal.

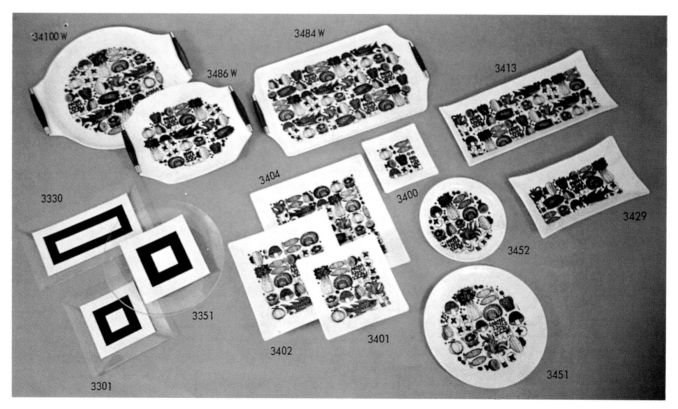

1.65 Melange on white aura bent glass.

36

1.66 White porcelainite plate with Melange pattern, 6" diameter. 5-10

1.67 Detail of Melange.

1.68 Detail of Melange.

1.70 White Porcelainite coffee percolator with polychrome Ambrosia, 9 3/4" height. 35-50

1.69 Contemporary photograph of Ambrosia coffee percolator on warming stand.

1.71 Lemon yellow Porcelainite coffee percolator with polychrome Coq D'or, 8 3/4" height. 35-50

1.72 White Porcelainite coffee percolator with Ambrosia pattern and matching mugs. 80-120 set

1.73 White Porcelainite coffee percolator with Green Garden pattern, 9" height plus warming stand. *Courtesy of Elinor Polster.* 35-50

1.74 White Porcelainite tray with Ambrosia (pineapple) pattern, 13 x 19". 25-40

1.75 White Porcelainite tray with Ambrosia, 11 1/2 x 16". 25-35

1.76 Detail.

1.77 White Porcelainite tray with Coq D'or pattern, 23" length. 25-40

1.78 White Porcelainite warming tray with Ambrosia pattern, 12" length without handles. 20-40

1.79 White Porcelainite casserole with cover and warming stand in Green Garden pattern, 5 3/8" height without stand, 7" diameter without handles. 35-50

1.80 Detail of Green Garden.

1.81 Detail of Green Garden.

BELOW:
1.83 Group of small flat bent glass plates in Seascape pattern in 22-karat gold and Hifire grey fused to opaque white opal glass, made by Glass Guild and introduced in 1957, 6 5/8 × 4 1/8". 10-15 each

Georges Briard

1.82 Detail of Green Garden.

1.84 Square serving plate with Seascape on white opal glass, 11 3/4" square. 35-50

1.85 Detail of Seascape.

1.86 Three-pocket serving plate with Seascape on white opal, in 1957 catalog, 13 x 22" Since the white opal glass is usually bent by hand, irregularities in size and shape are to be expected. 50-75

1.88 Detail of apple.

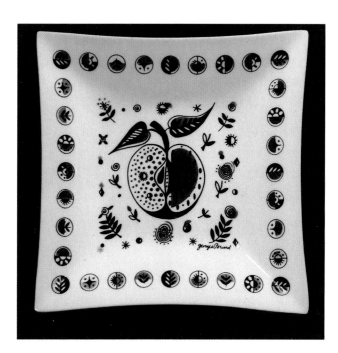

1.87 Square bent glass plate with Forbidden Fruit apple motif on white opal, 11 3/4" square. 35-50

1.89 Georges Briard signature with detail.

1.90 Detail of Forbidden Fruit border.

1.91 Square flat glass plate with Forbidden Fruit border design, 6" square. 6-8

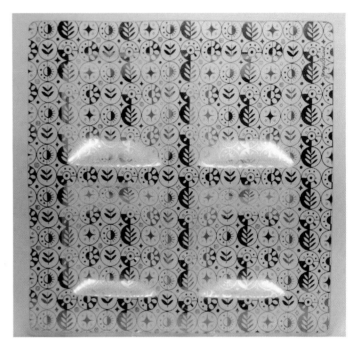

1.93 Four-pocket server with Forbidden Fruit border design, 15" square. 25-35

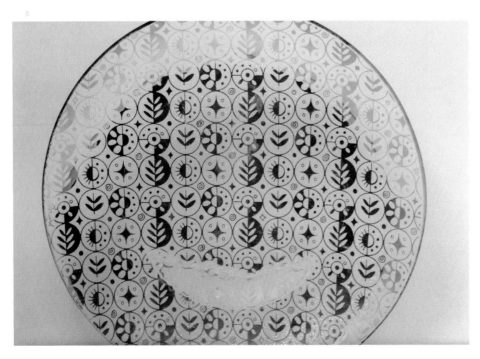

1.92 Round tray in clear aura with Forbidden Fruit border design, 12" diameter. 15-20

1.94 Group of white suburban glasses with Forbidden Fruit. 8-10 each

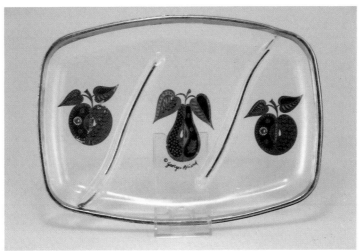

1.95 Three-part relish tray with orange and gold Forbidden Fruit. 10-15

1.96 Detail of pear.

1.97 Detail of apple.

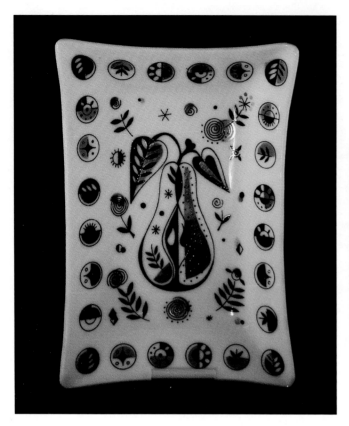

1.98 Shallow bowl with Forbidden Fruit on white opal glass, 5 3/4 x 8 1/4", an unusual example without a signature on the front but with a Glass Guild paper sticker on the back. 15-25

1.99 Circular serving tray with Forbidden Fruit on white opal glass and brass handle, 12 1/2" diameter. 35-50

1.100 Top view of circular tray.

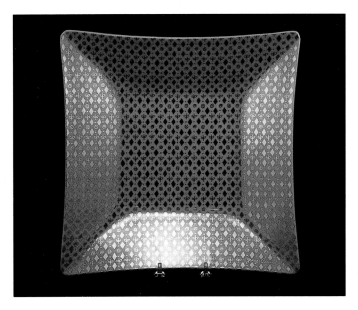

1.101 Square shallow bowl with overall diamond pattern on robin's egg blue glass, made by Glass Guild as a sample of the color but not commercially produced, 11 1/2" square.

1.102 Square shallow bowl with Persian Garden on robin's egg blue glass, made by Glass Guild as a sample and most likely one-of-a-kind, 11 1/2" square.

1.103 Detail of Persian Garden.

1.104 Glass Guild one-of-a-kind sample plates on robin's egg blue glass with Golden Harvest, left, and Seascape, right, each 6" square.

1.105 Golden Harvest pattern in hand burnished two-tone gold on white opal 6" plates. 12-18 each

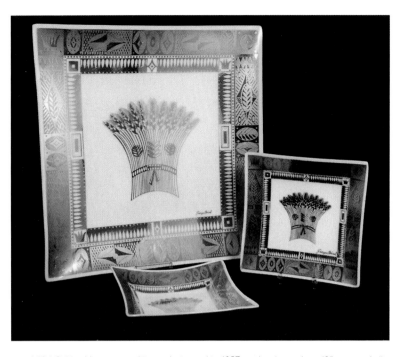

1.106 Golden Harvest on white opal, pictured in 1957 catalog: large plate, 12" square; shallow bowl, 5 3/4" square; flat plate, 6" square. 35-50; 15-20; 12-18

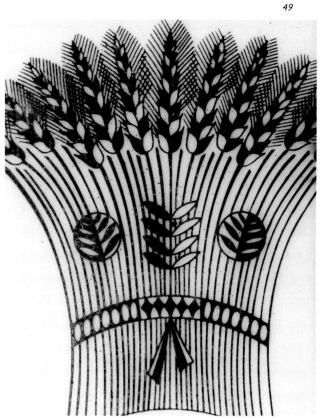

1.07 Detail of center.

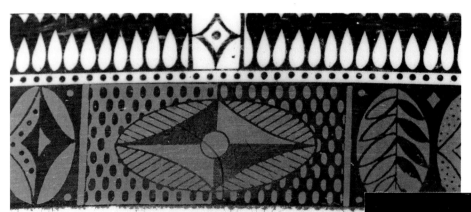

1.108 Detail of border.

1.109 White opal plate with depression in center for dip cup, with Golden Harvest border, 10" square. 25-35

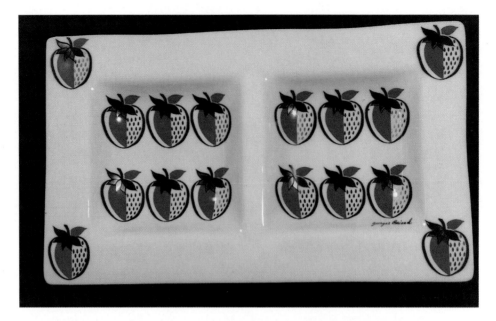

1.110 White opal glass two-pocket server with black and red strawberry pattern, 14 1/2 x 8 1/2". 35-50

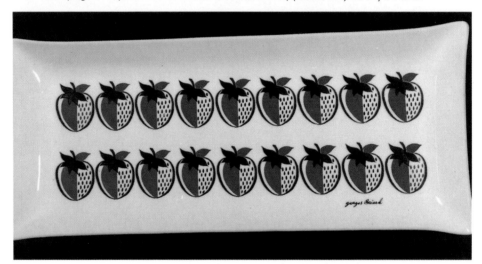

1.111 Long rectangular relish tray in white opal with black and red strawberries, 16 5/8 x 7 1/4". 35-50

1.112 Detail of strawberries.

1.113 Casserole in gold stippled glass and brass cover with white tile insert in Persian Garden pattern, pictured in 1957 catalog, 10" length, 3 5/8" height. 25-35

1.114 Square plate with gold Persian Garden pattern on clear aura, 11 3/4" square. 15-20

1.115 Persian Garden on clear aura glass: square shallow bowl, 5 3/4" square, and plate with Glass Guild signature, 6" square. 7-10 each

1.116 Rectangular tray with Persian Garden, 6 1/4 x 17 3/4". 15-20

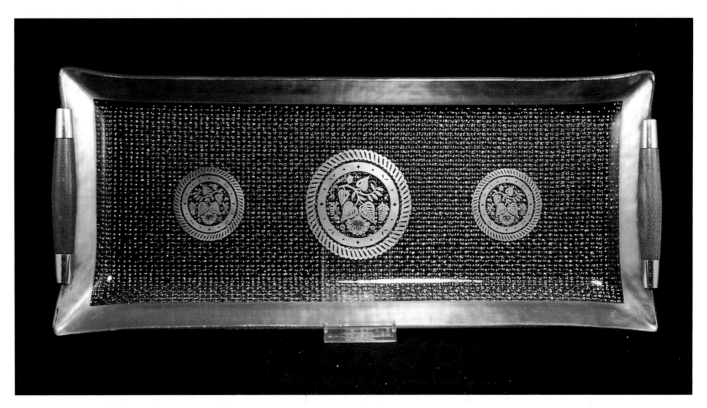

1.117 Rectangular tray with Silver Damask and wood handles, 7 x 16 3/4". 20-25

1.118 Oval four-part relish tray with Silver Damask pattern, 12 7/8" length. Since Silver Damask is made with sterling silver, the decoration will tarnish and clean like objects made of silver. 12-18

1.119 Detail of Silver Damask.

1.120 Three-part relish with Silver Damask. 10-15

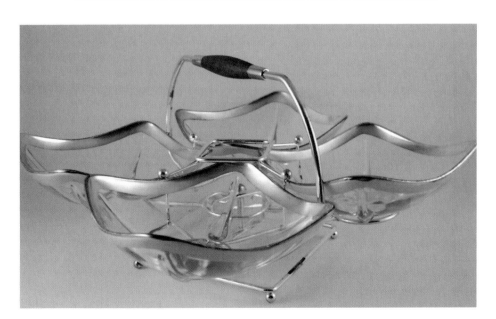

1.121 Four relish bowls with silver trim in metal holder with wood handle. 25-35

54

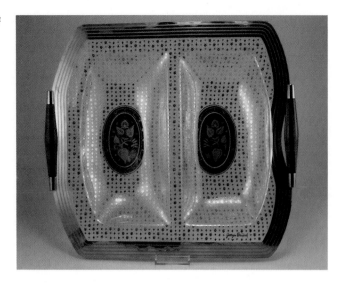

1.122 Two-pocket serving tray with wood and brass handles in Gold Damask, 14 1/2 x 13". 20-25

1.123 Square shallow bowl with gold Regalia pattern, shown in 1959 catalog, 5 3/4" square. 8-10

1.124 Suburban with Regalia. 5-7 each

1.125 Detail of Gold Damask.

1.126 Detail of Regalia.

1.127 Sonata pattern on 8" plate and 5" bowl, shown in 1960 catalog. 8-10 each

1.129 Detail of Sonata.

1.128 Detail of Sonata.

1.130 Square tray with Ambrosia on clear aura, 16 1/4" square. *Courtesy of Merv and Sylvia Glickman.* 20-30

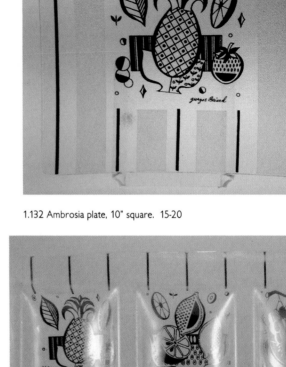

1.132 Ambrosia plate, 10" square. 15-20

1.133 Three-pocket server in variation of Ambrosia, 22 x 13". 30-40

1.131 Detail of Ambrosia.

1.134 Detail of Ambrosia.

1.135 Ice container with *Town & Country* pattern, 5" height, 5 3/4" diameter. 12-18

1.136 Detail.

1.137 Imperial Garden pattern on serving tray of flat glass with gold texture (gold painted on back) and wood and brass handles, shown in 1960 catalog, 12 1/4 x 10 1/4". 20-30

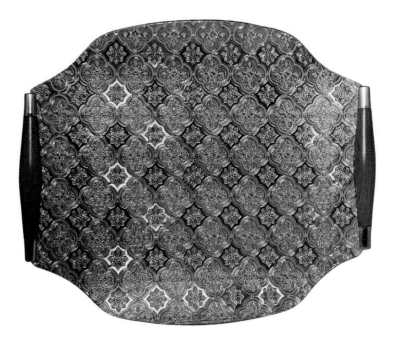

1.138 Pressed Iberia pattern on serving tray with wood and brass handles, 12 1/4 × 10 1/4". 20-30

1.139 Detail of Iberia.

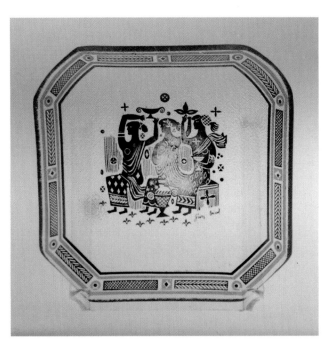

1.140 Olympia pattern in gold and claret on 6" plate, shown in 1958 catalog. 8-12

1.141 Detail of Olympia border.

1.142 Golden Celeste on chip 'n dip bowls, shown in 1957 catalog, 10" diameter large bowl. 25-35

1.143 Golden Celeste 12" square serving plate. *Courtesy of Elaine and Eli Friedman.* 20-30

1.144 Golden Celeste plate, 4 x 6 3/4". 8-10

Above:
1.145 Detail of Celeste.

1.146 Detail of Paradise.

1.147 Paradise pattern with turquoise and white birds on salad bowl, shown in 1960 catalog, 10 3/4" diameter. 15-25

1.149 Heritance shallow bowl, 7 1/2" diameter. 10-12

1.148 Paradise snack bowl with wood and brass center post for handle, 7" across, 8" height. 12-18

1.150 Cameo pattern detail.

1.151 Tumblers with gold and black Town & Country pattern. 8-10 each

1.152 Detail of Town & Country.

1.153 Hi ball glasses with Coq Rouge. 8-10 each

1.154 Detail of Coq Rouge.

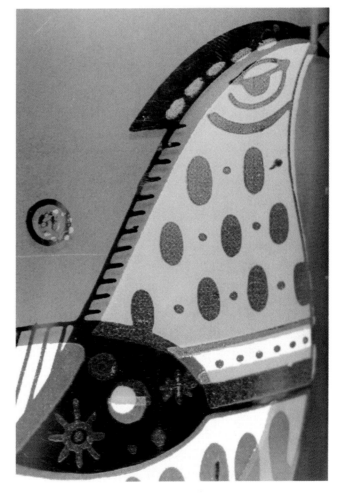

1.155 Detail of Coq Rouge.

1.156 Small white glasses with Chess pattern, 3" height. 6-8 each

1.157 Detail of Chess.

1.158 White tumblers with gold string instruments. 8-10 each

1.159 Suburban glasses with Wall Street pattern, in 1959 catalog. 6-8 each

1.160 Detail of Wall Street.

1.161 Suburban glasses with Tiara pattern. 4-7 each

1.162 Small glasses with orange, lime green, and gold fruit. 5-8 each

1.163 Roly poly glass with Rondo pattern, 1960s. 4-7

1.164 Bird in Cage martini mixer, 9 1/4" height. 15-20

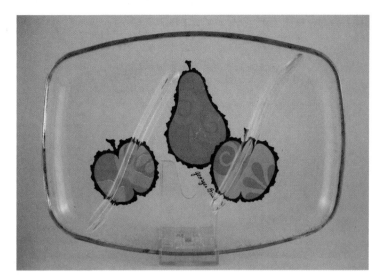

Above:
1.167 Orange Pageant on three-part relish tray, 10" length. *Courtesy of Merv and Sylvia Glickman.* 15-20

Right:
1.168 Mandarin Orange glass tray with Orange Pageant pattern of yellow and orange fruit, 11 3/4" square. 30-40

1.165 Butterfly on martini mixer, 9 1/4" height. 15-20

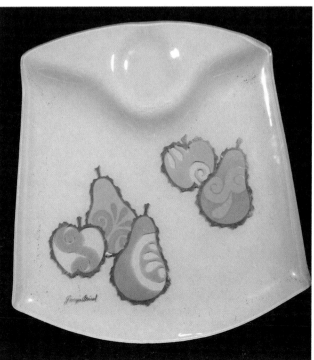

1.166 Detail of butterfly.

1.169 Peacock Blue tray with Blue Pageant blue and purple fruit, 13 1/4 x 12 3/4". 30-40

1.170 Hyalyn rectangular vase in white bisque with gold Facade decoration, 5 1/2" height, 5" width, 3" depth, early 1960s. 100-150

1.171 Detail of Facade.

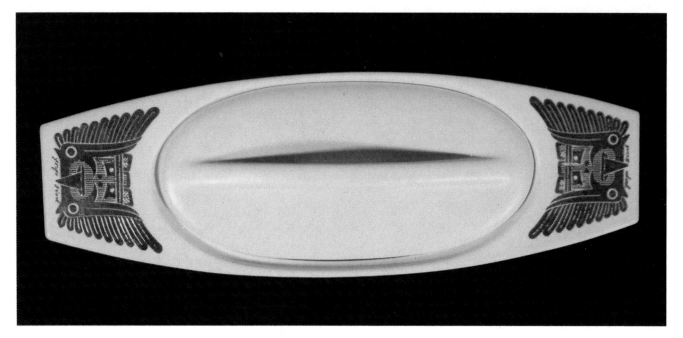

1.172 Hyalyn covered serving tray in white bisque with gold Pre-Columbian motif, cork applied to bottom marked "Georges Briard Midas for hyalyn," 14 5/8" length, early 1960s. 100-150

1.173 Detail (in focus, but gold applied over edge).

1.174 Hyalyn oval serving tray in white bisque with gold Cornucopia, cork applied to bottom with "Georges Briard Midas for hyalyn," 15 1/2" length, early 1960s. 80-120

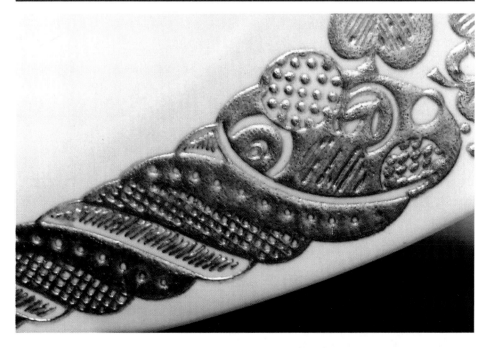

1.175 Detail of Cornucopia.

1.177 Detail of plant.

1.176 Hyalyn vase in white bisque porcelain with gold potted plant decoration in "Midas" series, 8" height, early 1960s. 100-150

1.178 Detail of pot.

Above:
1.179 Hyalyn
porcelain circular
ashtray in white
bisque with designs
in gold circles, 10"
diameter, early
1960s. 80-120

1.180 Detail.

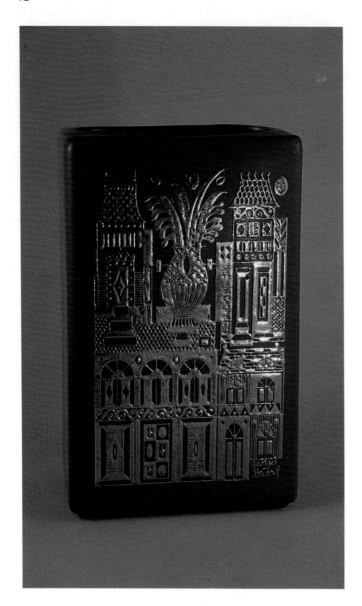

1.181 Hyalyn porcelain rectangular vase in brown bisque with gold Facade, 8" height, early 1960s. 125-175

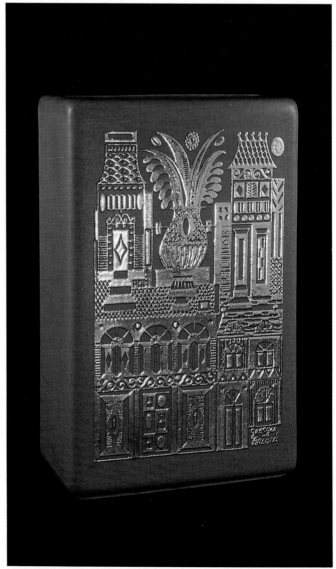

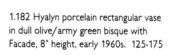

1.182 Hyalyn porcelain rectangular vase in dull olive/army green bisque with Facade, 8" height, early 1960s. 125-175

1.183 Detail of Facade.

1.184 Detail of Facade.

74

1.185 Lightolier 9145 rectangular base in dark brown bisque with gold Facade, early 1960s. 150-250

1.187 Lightolier 9142 lamp base in dark orange bisque with gold Forbidden Fruit, early 1960s. 150-250

1.186 Lightolier 9150 lamp base in dark brown bisque with gold bird and plant, early 1960s. 150-250

1.188 Lightolier 0146 lamp base in white bisque with gold rooster, early 1960s. 150-250

1.189 Linometric pattern on ceramic coffee server, 9 3/4" height. 25-35

1.190 Linometric ceramic casserole with brass-plated cover, 6" height, 11 3/4" across. 25-35

76

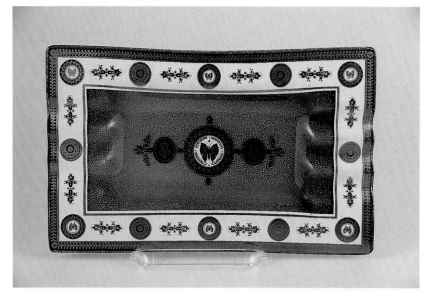

1.191 Ashtray with Embassy
pattern in gold and white on
aura glass with dark teal green
backing, 6 1/2 x 10 1/2".
25-35

1.192 Detail of butterfly.

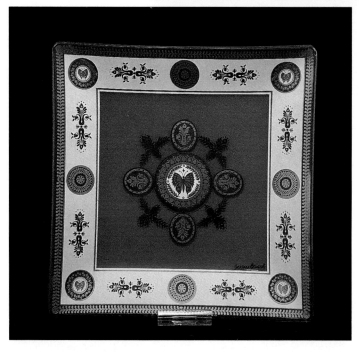

1.193 Ashtray with Embassy pattern in gold and white on aura glass with vivid
orange backing, 7 1/2" square. 25-35

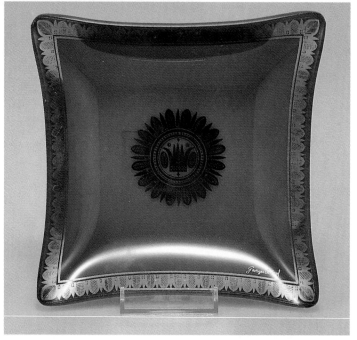

1.194 Plate with Regalia pattern and dark teal backing, 5 3/4" square. 20-25

1.195 Hand-decorated gold toleware 8-sided tray with chess knight, signed Geo Briard, 8 1/2" length. 25-35

1.196 Heaven Can Wait linen cocktail napkins in original box, 7 x 5 1/4" average. 40-50 set

1.197 Detail of Heaven Can Wait.

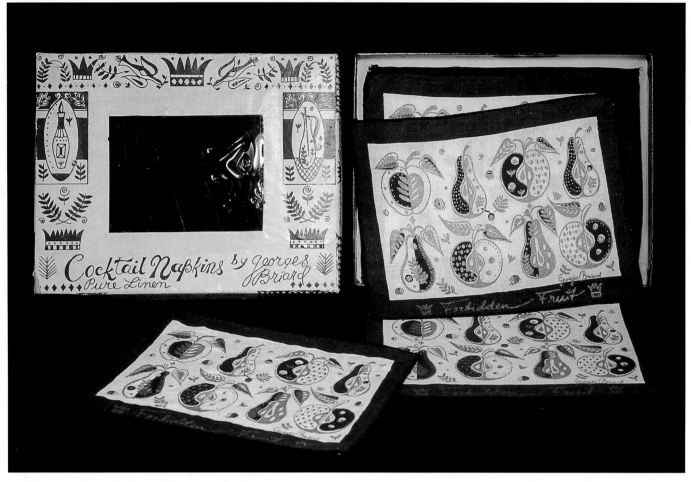

1.198 Forbidden Fruit linen cocktail napkins in original box. 40-50 set

1.199 Butterflies linen cocktail napkins in original box. 40-50 set

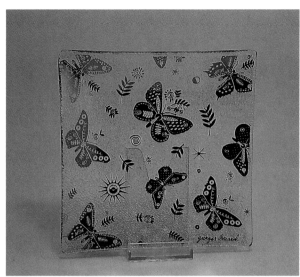

1.200 Plate with Butterflies, 6" square. 8-10

Below:
1.201 Smoke grey glass canape plates with insects and leaves, 4 x 6 5/8" in original box. 50-75 set

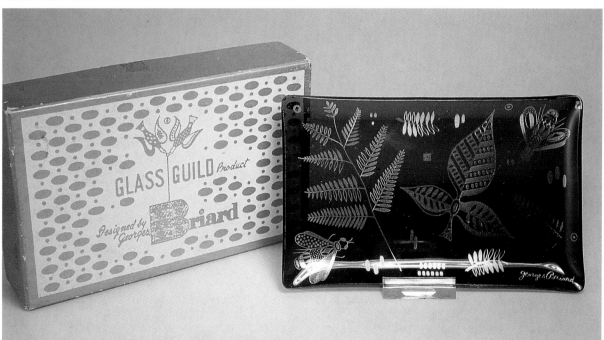

1.202 Square 6" plates with insect pattern on smoke grey glass. *Courtesy of Elaine and Eli Friedman.* 10-15 each

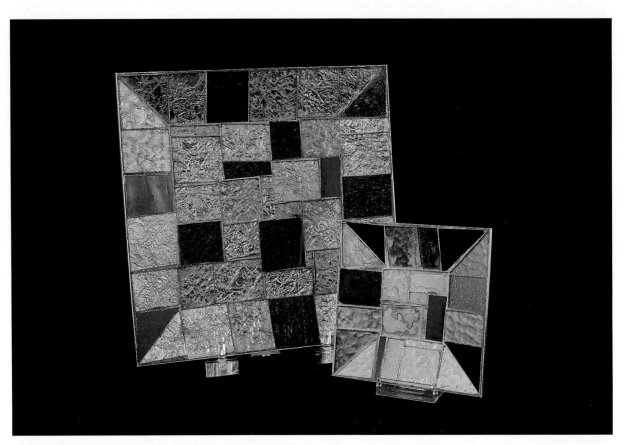

1.203 Green and blue glass mosaic on anodized aluminum plates: left, 9 3/4" square; right, 5" square. 50-60; 20-25

1.204 Green and blue glass mosaic on anodized aluminum plates: left, 7 3/4" square; right, 8 1/4 x 5 3/4". 35-45; 30-40

1.205 Clock with green and blue glass mosaic, 12" square. 100-150

1.206 Left, wood cigarette box with glass mosaic in blues and greens, 5 5/8 x 3 5/8"; right, anodized aluminum ashtray with matching glass mosaic, 5" square. 40-50; 20-25

1.207 Detail of mosaic.

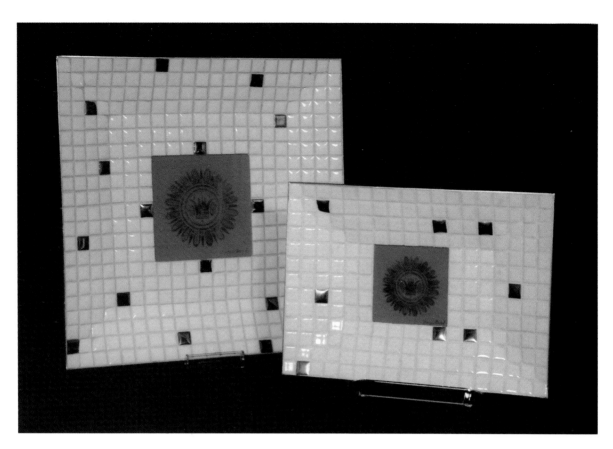

1.208 Mosaic ashtrays with white ceramic tiles and randomly placed gold tiles on anodized aluminum with glass insert: large, 9 5/8" square; small, 8 1/4 x 6". 40-50; 25-35

1.209 Detail of Regalia pattern on Mandarin Orange glass insert.

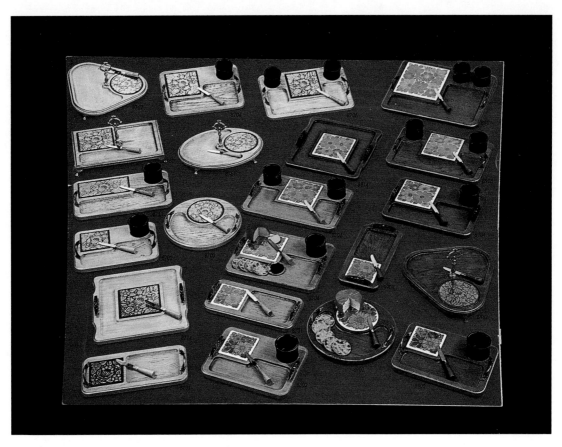

1.210 Cheese boards with Town & Country Silver and Flower tile inserts.

1.211 Walnut servers with ceramic tile inserts: TL 2-dip 13 1/2" square board with 6" tile; CL 8 x 16" board with 6" tile; BL 6 1/2 x 14" board with 4" tile; TLC 1-dip 12" square board with 6" tile; C 7 1/2 x 13" board with 6" round tile; BC 1-dip 9" square board with 4" tile; TRC 1-dip 11 x 12 1/2" board with 4" tile; CR 7 1/4 x 14" board with 4" tile; BR 4-compartment board with 6" round tile; TR 7 1/2" square board with 6" round tile and dome.

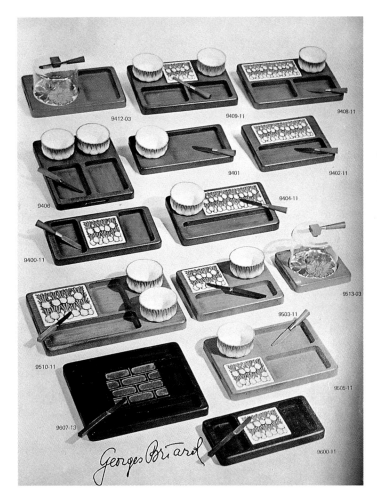

1.212 Serving trays and cheese boards with ceramic tile inserts: Onion pattern tile on Crisp Green and Golden Yellow wood boards, and Chateau tile on Country French (Darkwood) boards.

Below:
1.213 Oak cheese and dip boards with Spanish Gold tile inserts: TL 2-dip 12 x 16" board with 6" tile; CL 1-dip 9 1/2 x 13" board with 4" tile; BL 9 1/2 x 15" board with 4 x 8" tile; TC warmer; C 1-dip 11 x 14" board with 6" tile; TR 1-dip 10 x 16" board with 4 x 8" tile; CR 6 1/2 x 14" board with 4" tile; BR 7 1/2 x 14" board with 6" round tile with dome.

86

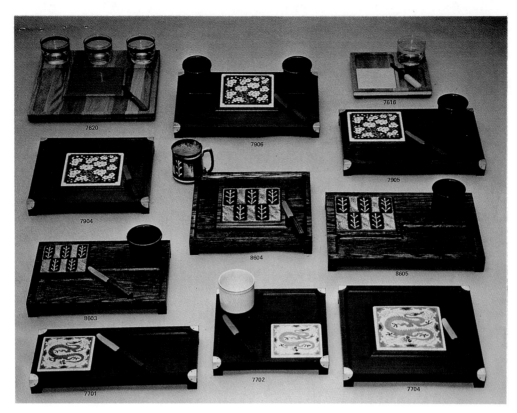

1.214 Servers and boards: TL 3-dip 14" square board with 6" Patio Orange tile; TCL 12" square board with 6" Chinese Floral tile; BCL 1-dip 9 1/2 x 12 1/2" oak board with 4" Briar tile; BL 6 1/2 x 14" board with 4" Dragon tile; TC 2-dip 10 1/2 x 16" board with 6" Chinese Floral tile; C 12" square oak board with 6" Briar tile; BC 1-dip 10" square board with 4" Dragon tile; TR 1-dip 9" square board with 4" Patio Yellow tile; TCR 1-dip 11 x 14" board with 6" Chinese Floral tile; BCR 1-dip 11 x 14" oak board with 6" Briar tile; BR 12" square board with 6" Dragon tile.

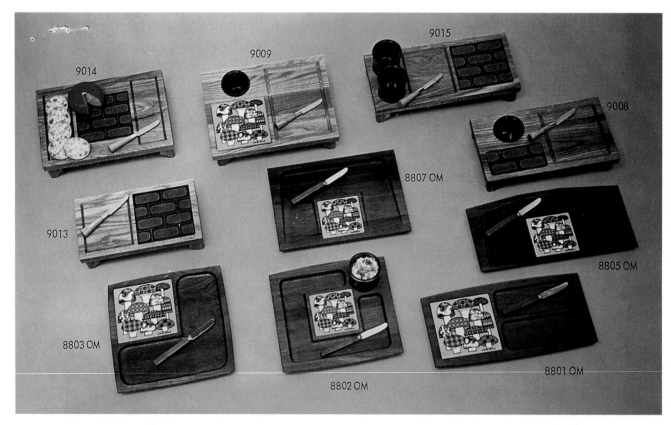

1.215 Servers and boards with Mushroom tile inserts.

1.216 Top: wood servers in Antique Green with Green Wildflower inserts; bottom: Elegance with Orange Flower tile inserts.

1.217 Antique White servers with Town & Country tile inserts: T 11 x 15 board with square tile; L 14" triangular board with round tile; B 14 1/2" round board with round tile; R gourmet ladder, 21 x 12 x 9 1/2" with round tile.

1.218 Cheese board with 6" ceramic tile insert with Ambrosia, 16 x 7 1/2" board. 35-45

1.220 One-dip cheese board with enamel tile insert in Melange pattern. 20-30

1.219 Detail of Ambrosia.

1.221 One-dip cheese server with 4 1/2" Orange Flower enamel tile insert, 12 x 11" board. 20-30

1.222 Detail of Orange Flower.

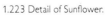

1.224 Two-dip double cheese board with 6" Sunflower enamel tile insert, 15 x 12 3/4" board. 25-35

1.223 Detail of Sunflower.

1.225 Double cheese board with 4 × 8" Galaxy enamel tile insert, 15 × 9 1/2" board. 20-30

Below:
1.227 Cheese board with 4 1/2" Facade enamel tile insert, 11 3/4 × 11 1/4" board. 20-30

1.226 Detail of Galaxy.

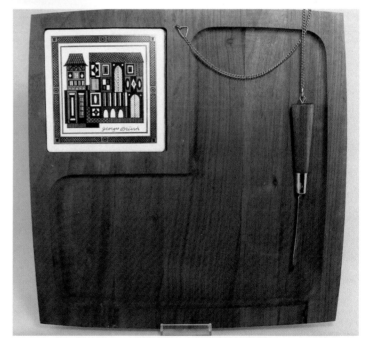

1.228 Detail of Facade.

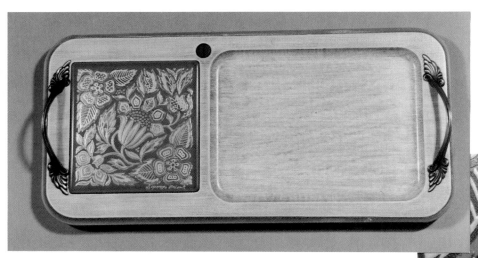

1.229 Handled cheese board with 4 1/2" enamel tile insert in Town & Country Silver, 14 x 6 1/2" board. 20-30

1.230 Detail of Town & Country.

1.231 Gold Town & Country tile on cheese board, 8 3/4" square. 20-30

1.232 Cheese board with 4 x 8" enamel tile insert with wide gold border. 15-25

1.233 One-dip cheese board with 4 1/2" Spanish Gold enamel tile insert, 13 x 9 1/2" board. 15-25

1.234 Detail of Spanish Gold.

1.235 Cheese boards with 6" and 4 1/2 " Eldorado enameled metal tile inserts, a version of Forbidden Fruit; small board 8 3/4" square; large board 14 x 9" with gold metal pear attached. 15-20; 35-45

1.236 Detail of pear.

1.237 Detail of gold metal pear.

1.238 Eldorado gold pear on white porcelain dish. 50-75

1.239 Cheese board with Sonata tile insert. 15-25

1.240 Round handled tray with gold backing and Sonata on front. 30-40

1.241 Detail of Sonata.

1.242 Hot Butler with Sonata, 9 1/4 x 14 1/4" plus handles. 10-15

1.243 African Safari ice buckets, tumblers, and cheese boards from late 1960s-1970s

1.244 Black and white Op Art design on clear glass serving pieces, late 1960s.

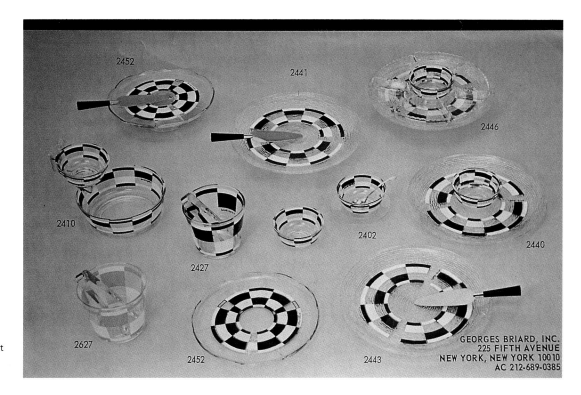

2452 2441 2446 2410 2427 2402 2440 2627 2452 2443

GEORGES BRIARD, INC.
225 FIFTH AVENUE
NEW YORK, NEW YORK 10010
AC 212-689-0385

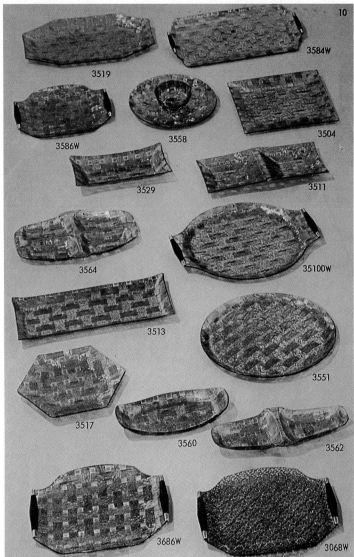

1.245 Formed glass serving trays from Jan. 1969 catalog.

1.246 Drinkware from Jan. 1969 catalog.

1.247 Page from 1969 catalog.

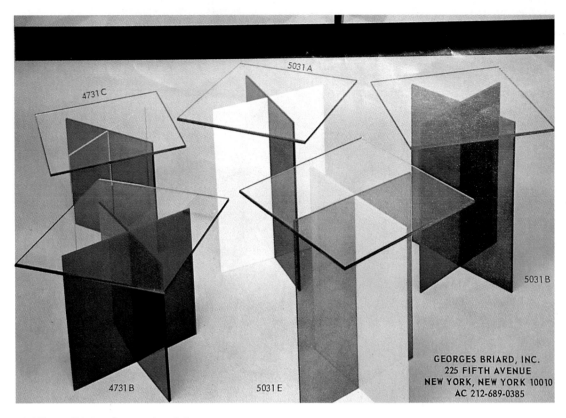

1.248 Tables of Modern Geometry, late 1960s.

1.249 Modern Geometry accent tables from back cover of Jan. 1969 catalog.

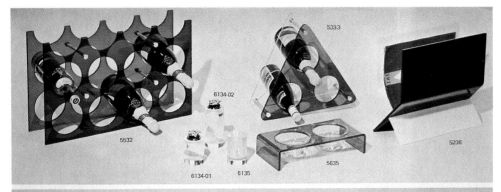

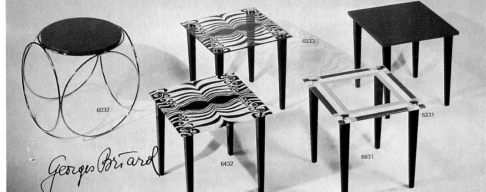

1.250 Top: lucite wine racks, butane lighters, magazine rack; bottom: glass-top wooden-leg tables in Futura, Square Red, and Stripes, with vinyl-top wire-hoop table (left).

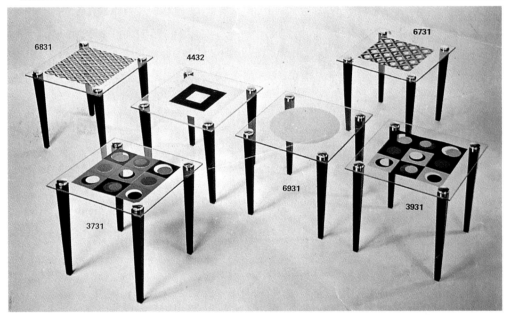

1.251 Accent tables: BL Eclipse Red, TL Optical Black & White, TC Chrome Mirror Square, C Chrome Mirror Circle, TR Eclipse Yellow, BR Illusion Black & White.

1.252 Accent tables in solid colors and Melange pattern.

1.253 Glasses with Carrara pattern. 4-7 each

1.254 Further Psychedelic Acid
Test for Drop Ins, late 1960s.
These are part of a set of
fourteen glasses (lot #101)
that sold for $650 at the
Sotheby's "Collectors'
Carrousel" auction held in
New York on December 15,
1993. *Courtesy of Jean O.
Mueller.*

1.255 Detail.

1.256 Golf old fashioned
glasses, 1970s. 5-7 each

1.257 Drinkware from 1970s. 4-7 each

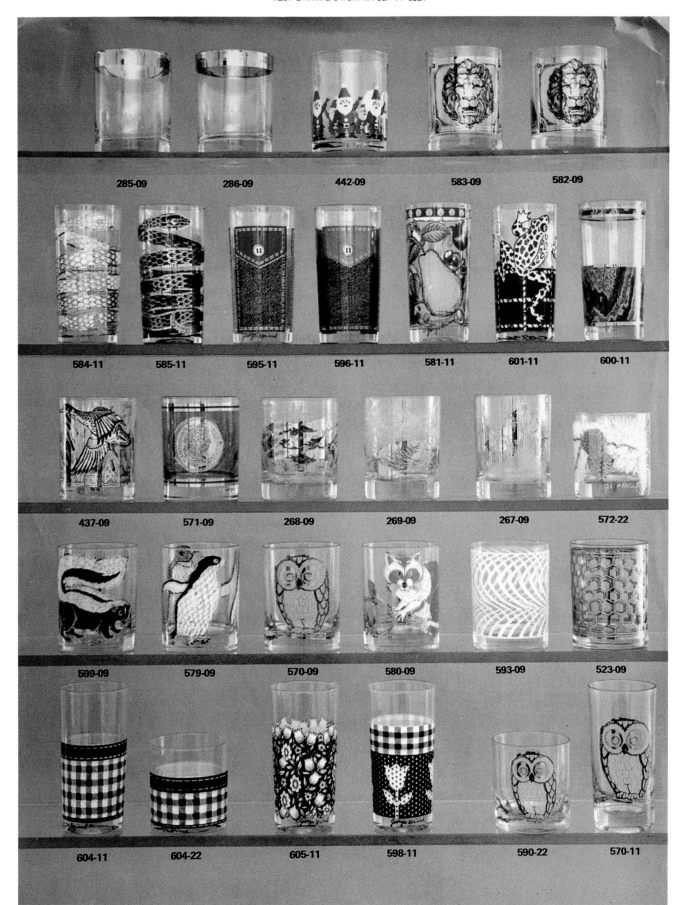

285-09 286-09 442-09 583-09 582-09

584-11 585-11 595-11 596-11 581-11 601-11 600-11

437-09 571-09 268-09 269-09 267-09 572-22

599-09 579-09 570-09 580-09 593-09 523-09

604-11 604-22 605-11 598-11 590-22 570-11

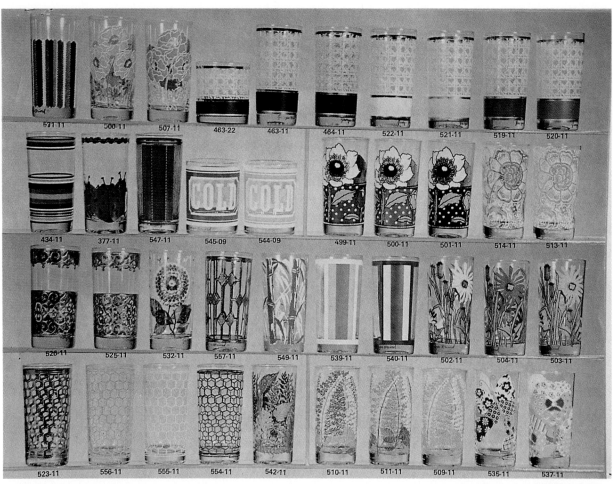

571-11 500-11 507-11 463-22 463-11 464-11 522-11 521-11 519-11 520-11

434-11 377-11 547-11 545-09 544-09 499-11 500-11 501-11 514-11 513-11

526-11 525-11 532-11 557-11 549-11 539-11 540-11 502-11 504-11 503-11

523-11 556-11 555-11 554-11 542-11 510-11 511-11 509-11 535-11 537-11

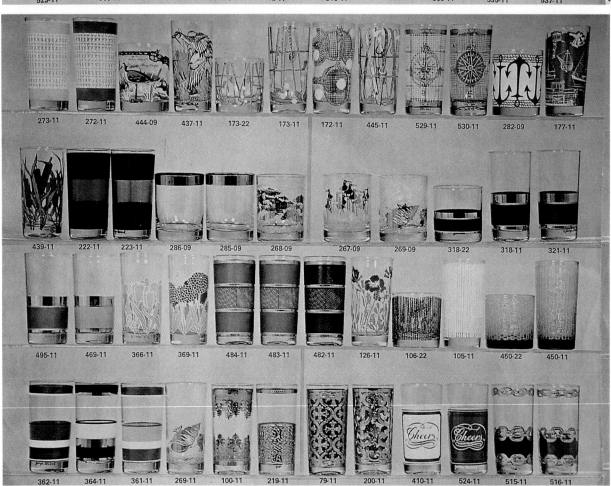

273-11 272-11 444-09 437-11 173-22 173-11 172-11 445-11 529-11 530-11 282-09 177-11

439-11 222-11 223-11 286-09 285-09 268-09 267-09 269-09 318-22 318-11 321-11

495-11 469-11 366-11 369-11 484-11 483-11 482-11 126-11 106-22 105-11 450-22 450-11

362-11 364-11 361-11 269-11 100-11 219-11 79-11 200-11 410-11 524-11 515-11 516-11

Opposite page, top:
1.258 Drinkware from 1970s. Top row left to right: Brando Stripe, Anemone Yellow, Anemone Green, Cane Black, Cane Black, Cane Brown, Cane White, Cane Yellow, Cane Green, Cane Orange; second row: Stripes Red, Ladybug, Sentinel Red, Cold Orange, Cold Yellow, Polka Poppy Blue, Polka Poppy Orange, Polka Poppy Black, Frost Flower Lime, Frost Flower Yellow; third row: Madrid Rose, Madrid Lime, Moonflower Gold, Stainglass Lime & Gold, Bamboo Orange, Rally Orange, Rally Blue, Tigerlily White, Tigerlily Orange, Tigerlily Yellow; bottom row: Gold Wire, Wire Ice Yellow, Wire Ice White, Wire Ice Black, Jungle Gold, Fern Orange, Fern Green, Fern Yellow, Butterfly, Pansy. 4-7 each

Opposite page, bottom:
1.259 Drinkware from 1970s. Top row left to right: Straw Yellow, Straw Orange, Decoy, Geese, Golf Gold, Golf Gold, Tennis Gold, Ski Gold, Captain White, Captain Blue, Anchors, Nautical; second row: Marshweed, Kudo Blue, Kudo Avocado, Silver Band, Gold Band, Fish Gold, Gull Gold, Shell Gold, Metric Gold & Black, Metric Gold & Brown; third row: Chromatic Brown, Chromatic Yellow, Tulip Yellow, Zinnia Red, Goldnet Green, Goldnet Brown, Goldnet Black, Field Flower, Icicle Black, Icicle White, Smoke Ice, Smoke Ice; bottom row: Cabana Red, Cabana Black, Cabana Orange, Shell, Duchess, Marac Gold, Firenze Gold, Spanish Gold, Cheers, Cheers Blue, Chain Black, Chain Brown. 4-7 each

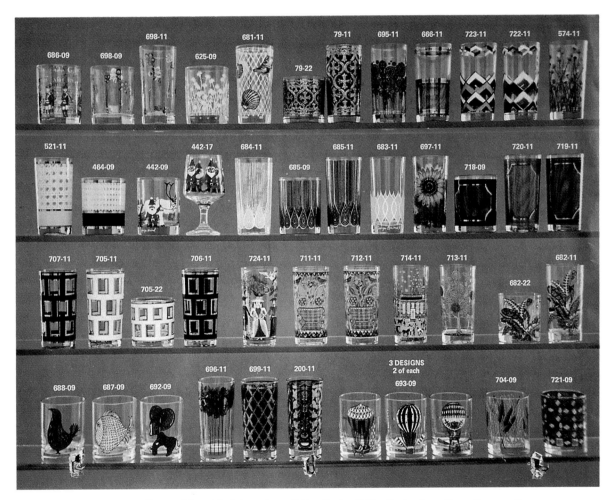

1.260 Glassware from Fall 1974. Top row left to right: Independence, Golden Garden, Golden Garden, Straw Flower, Seascape, Firenze, Firenze, Study in Brown, Fusion, Art Deco Black, Art Deco Brown, Strawflowers; second row: Cane Yellow, Cane Brown, Santa, Santa, Peacock White, Peacock Brown, Peacock Brown, Teardrop, Sunflower, Stitched Leather Black, Stitched Leather Teak, Stitched Leather Brown; third row: Windows Brown, Windows White, Windows Black, Military Wedding, Greenfield Hill Orange, Greenfield Hill Blue, The Town, Tree of Life, Feather Bouquet; bottom row: Bird, Fish, Mouse, Harvest, Harlequin Brown, Spanish Gold, Balloons, Balloons, Balloons, Wildlife, Weave Brown. 4-7 each

1.261 Drinkware from 1970s/80s. 4-7 each

1.262 Drinkware from 1970s/80s. 4-7 each

Above: 1.263 Drinkware from 1970s/80s. 4-7 each
Below: 1.264 Drinkware from 1970s/80s. 4-7 each

1.265 Art Deco revival in black, grey and white, 1970s-80s. 5-7 each

1.266 White striped old fashioned glasses, 1970s-80s. 4-6 each

ANNIVERSARY EDITION			
1235	Pear Salt/Pepper	12	3.00	2.50
1236	Apple Salt/Pepper	12	3.00	2.50
1240	10½" Plate Each	12	10.00	9.50
1241	7½" Cake Plate, s/4	12	14.50	14.00
1243	Mug, s/4	12	14.50	14.00

1.267 Special Anniversary Edition 1959-1979 Forbidden Fruit in Black and Gold.

1.268 Private Collection china dinnerware from late 1970s and early 1980s. La Salade, 1980.

1.269 Private Collection china dinnerware, Secrets of the Sea.

1.270 Private Collection china dinnerware, L'Art Nouveau.

1.272 Private Collection china dinnerware, Royal Tapestry (called Imperial Brocade if rust color), inspired by 19th-century Japanese Kutani porcelain.

1.271 Private Collection china dinnerware, Oriental Peacock, inspired by 19th-century Oriental porcelain.

1.273 Private Collection china dinnerware, Imperial Malachite, 1980.

1.274 Cover of 1985 catalog with Memphasis: Stripes, Spots, Pyramid, Sunburst.

1.275 Page from 1985 catalog. Top: formed glass pocket servers; bottom: ice buckets, trays, and other barware.

1.276 Drinkware from 1985
catalog. 4-6 each

1.277 Drinkware from 1985
catalog. 4-6 each

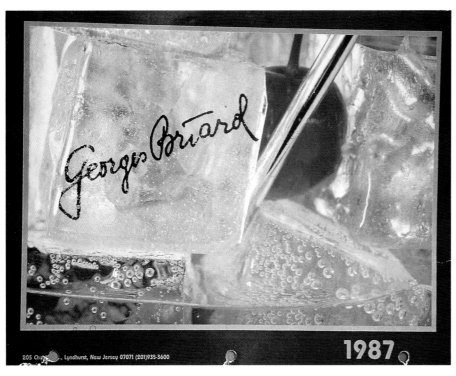

1.278 Cover of 1987 catalog.

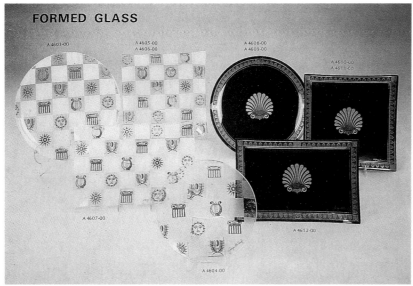

1.279 Formed glass from 1988 catalog with designs based on Neoclassical and shell motifs from the 1950s.

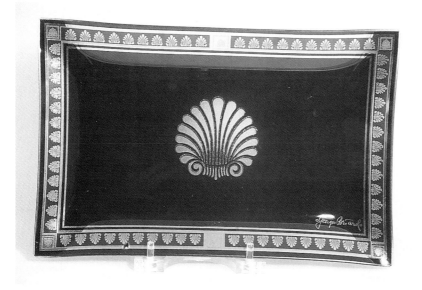

1.280 Rectangular plate with black enamel backing, decorated with gold Neoclassical shell, 8 7/8 x 13 3/4", signed © Georges Briard ®. 20-25

1.281 Drinkware from 1988 catalog. 4-6 each

1.282 Circus ice buckets and tumblers, 1970s.

1.283 Coasters, 1980s.

1.284 Coasters, 1980s.

1.285 China plate from 1970s printed on the back "Topiary Wreath, a fanciful holiday celebration designed and signed by Georges Briard," 7 5/8" diameter. 8-12

1.286 Detail of tree.

1.287 Detail of wreath.

1.288 Late 1980s Evergreen Group product: Floating Glass Caddies for pool or hot tub—vinyl Caddy depicting Baseball, Tennis, Soccer, and Beach Ball, with 10-oz. acrylic glass.

1.289 Late 1980s Evergreen Group Al Fresco stoneware microwave-to-oven-to-table cookware with life-like graphics.

1.290 Evergreen Group barware and serving accessories in Aristocrat pattern, 1989.

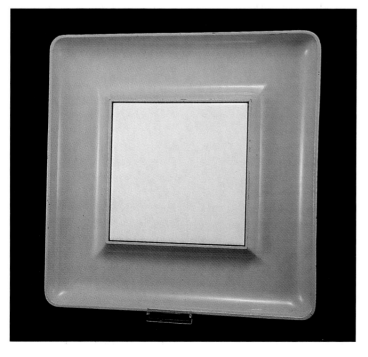

1.291 Lime green "lacquered" plastic tray, 12" square, with 6" white ceramic tile insert. Paper sticker on back reads BOUTIQUE SERIES AN ORIGINAL DESIGN BY GEORGES BRIARD J & H INTERNATIONAL JAPAN. 10-15

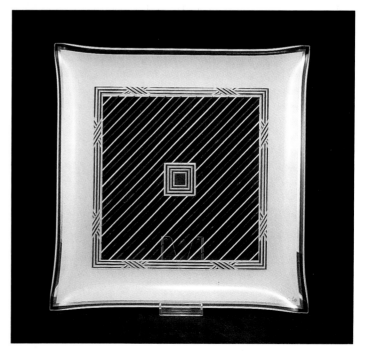

1.292 Aristocrat plate, 11 1/4" square, and one of the latest items produced (1989). 10-15

Chapter Two
Sascha Brastoff

Sascha Brastoff was colorful, creative, and flamboyant, and his pottery designs reflect this. Words like theatrical, exotic, and even bizarre come to mind when encountering his prancing horses or Siamese dancers. Although the pottery shapes are usually modern, often freeform, and typically fifties, it is the decoration with its often subtle color schemes, gold accents, and handpainted signature on the front of each piece that catches the eye and identifies the ware. Brastoff produced both pottery and china dinnerware, but rather than emphasizing these place settings and matching tabletop accessories as other American pottery manufacturers of the period did, he preferred small to oversized vases and plates, smoking items, and figurines destined to decorate kidney-shaped cocktail tables and Danish Modern shelves. It was production pottery because it was factory made in pre-determined designs, but Brastoff's creations were also art pottery with the decoration painted by hand assuring that no two pieces were exactly alike. Advertisements, and Brastoff, declared that each piece was an original. In a 1958 interview with *The Cleveland Plain Dealer* he said, "It is more difficult to turn out an ashtray for five dollars than a display piece for $3,000...but why shouldn't everybody live with beautiful things?" Like the pottery, it was said that Sascha Brastoff was an original.

Born in Cleveland, Ohio in 1918, Samuel Brastoff (Brastofsky) was one of eight children (five were from his father's previous marriage). Before emigrating to the United States, his father Louis was a cutter in a Russian clothing factory; his mother Rebecca was from Hungary. Sammy decorated his first pottery as a toddler, but these early dinnerware decorations were always washed away in order to serve dinner. As he grew up, interest in painting turned more toward sculpture. He also studied ballet and, with a little coaxing from a Russian ballet teacher, took the name Sascha. His mother disapproved and continued to call him Sammy. Later, Sascha's talent as a dancer and entertainer would be his ticket out of an Army mechanical job and into Special Services where he earned the nickname "the G. I. Carmen Miranda." His costume for the popular Miranda act included an army blanket skirt, barracks bag turban with metal mess hall utensils for fruit, and sergeant's stripe earrings. Later, Sascha would meet Carmen Miranda and design both her personal and professional costumes.

After graduating from Glenville High School in Cleveland in 1935, he went to New York and found a job with Macy's department store doing window display. In his spare time, Sascha worked in ceramics. When he returned home to Cleveland, his sister Evelyn (Leftofsky) saved pennies from her household budget to pay for carfare so that Sascha could attend the Cleveland School of Art.

Clay sculpture was one of his early successes, and a piece was awarded a prize for whimsy in the 1939 Ceramic National exhibit at the Syracuse Museum of Art (Everson). For the 1948 Ceramic National he entered six canape trays with strange surreal decorations and titles like *Night Rider, Fish Monster,* and *Sex Monster.* He won best in show for pottery, and the trays are still on exhibit at the Everson Museum. In 1941 the Clay Club Gallery at 4 West 8th Street in New York presented his "Whimsies" in a one-man show from May 3 to June 7. In the printed program Sahl Swarz applauded Brastoff for both his fantastic imagination and the technical skill evidenced in terra cotta sculptures called whimsies. "Only one who is a sculptor at heart could model forms so fundamentally well-proportioned and graceful in composition..." Swarz also wrote, "Sascha Brastoff was born in Bangkok, Siam; Petrograd, Russia; or in Cleveland, Ohio depending on a mood or occasion...he lives in a world akin to that of Alice in Wonderland, where time is endless." Fish-mouthed figures and plump nudes were modeled in tinted clay, so rather than apply a glaze, Sascha achieved an unusual color effect with a natural matte finish.

One of the most well-received pieces in the show, *Europa and the Bull,* demonstrated both a strong Cleveland School and Austrian influence. In the 1920s and 1930s, clay sculpture was an important and popular artform with students and faculty at the Cleveland School of Art. Those who had studied in Austria brought a sophisticated yet whimsical style to an institution that was in the process of forming an artistic identity. Cowan Pottery collaborated with most of these ceramic artists, several of whom also used the Europa theme. Other titles from Brastoff's group of 37 whimsies listed in the exhibit program—*Faun Baby, Europa Etcetera, Neptune's Folly, Snake Charmer, Afrique, Lady Godiva,* and *Leda*—also suggest images similar to those of the Austrian-influenced Cleveland School. All of the pieces in the exhibit were sold to collectors or museums, and the event received national publicity in magazines such as *Time, Life, Harper's Bazaar,* and *Art Digest.*

The memorable appearance as Carmen Miranda in the Army's "Winged Victory" show in 1944 would be the last time Brastoff would see his parents for many years. Although he would return to Cleveland to promote or show his work (Higbee's Department Store often featured his pottery and ran newspaper ads) California would be his new home. His first job in California was with 20th Century Fox designing costumes, and he continued to work in ceramics in his spare time making things like dog and cat dishes for movie stars.

In 1947 Sascha opened his first ceramic plant on Sepulveda Blvd. in West Los Angeles and began making handpainted earthenware.

All pieces painted by Brastoff were signed "Sascha Brastoff," and those done under his supervision by one of several decorators trained to paint in his style were signed "Sascha B." All designs were Brastoff originals, and he personally approved the work decorated by his staff. Some of the artists he employed, notably Matthew Adams (Alaska line) and Marc Bellaire (exotic dancers), left the company and established their own studios. After meeting Winthrop Rockefeller (grandson of John D. Rockefeller) and gaining financial backing, Sascha opened a larger plant at 6300 Compton Ave. in Los Angeles, but it burned down only a few months later in July of 1952. Once again, with Rockefeller's backing, a new plant was built at 11520 West Olympic Blvd. in Los Angeles. The architects A. Quincy Jones and Frederick Emmons designed a modern glass and steel state of the art building with 35,000 square feet of floor space. It was recognized for excellence by the Southern California chapter of the American Institute of Architects (AIA) in 1954. The larger half-million-dollar facility covered a city block and by the late 1950s employed about one hundred pottery workers. Among the guests at the factory dedication in 1953 were Zsa Zsa Gabor, Edward G. Robinson, and Mitzi Gaynor. At that time the rooster backstamp in gold or platinum came into use.

Glass designer Winslow Anderson sometimes met Brastoff at ceramic and glass trade shows, such as in Pittsburgh, where he said Brastoff's booth gave new meaning to the word chaos. "Talk about care for madness!" Anderson added. Brastoff loved the wonderful modern glass Anderson designed for Blenko Glass in Milton, West Virginia, so they would trade big (expensive) gilded talc roosters for big colored glass bottles. The only problem with Brastoff's product was that the cheap talc body combined with a low firing temperature made it very soft. According to Anderson, "If you yelled too loudly, it would break." Yet, the decoration was appealing and well executed, and the company was very successful.

Even at the height of Brastoff's commercial pottery venture he continued to sculpt. In 1955 his "Sculpture in Steel" exhibit attracted seventeen patrons who were listed in a printed brochure; among the celebrities were Joan Crawford, Mr. and Mrs. Edward G. Robinson, and Winthrop Rockefeller. The style of these intriguing figural works was unmistakably Sascha; titles such as *Sea Ballet, Sun Rooster, Owl God,* and *Demon* were almost predictable and in keeping with Brastoff's love of fantasy. One, entitled *Prehistoric Fish,* was described in the brochure as having "individually hammered copper scales, each encrusted with swirls of pink bronze woven together in a network, contrasted with head and tail of black steel." His vocabulary of pink, black, and gold pottery decoration was cleverly translated onto metal.

Around 1960 a variety of factors, such as overconfidence from the quick success, led to an overextended company and financial losses. After suffering a nervous breakdown, Brastoff retired from the company in 1963, leaving Gerald Schwartz to carry on as plant manager, Ted Campbell as president, and Eddie Kourishima as art director. From 1964 to 1973 the plant operated at 12530 Yukon Ave. in Hawthorne, California without Brastoff. After a brief disappearance, Brastoff gradually recovered and re-entered the art world. Sculpture once again occupied Brastoff's time, and in 1966 he had

fifty pieces of metal sculpture in a one-man show at the Dalzell Hatfield Galleries in Los Angeles. He had remained friends with the Rockefellers, and Mrs. Winthrop Rockefeller hosted the event. The show was also seen at the Ross Widen Gallery in Cleveland in 1967. A significant departure from clay whimsies and earlier metal figures, the theme and title was "Moon-Age Sculpture." The result of five years of experimentation with various metals and techniques, many of the works were in silver-white magnesium. This was a new material for a work of art, and Brastoff gained a reputation as an innovator. He experimented in many materials, and in addition to sculpture and ceramics, during his long artistic career made jewelry of gold and gems, enameled on copper in the same decorative style as the pottery, designed fabric, painted, worked with glass, and eventually experimented with holograms. During the 1970s he collaborated with several companies to produce special lines, such as pottery for Haeger Pottery of Dundee, Illinois, scratchboard drawings on foil for Marina Metal Arts Co. of Marina del Rey, California, jewelry for Merle Norman Cosmetics, and miniature sculpture "Silver Circus" series for the Franklin Mint of Franklin Center, Pennsylvania.

After a struggle with prostate cancer, Sascha Brastoff died in Los Angeles in February of 1993, leaving a legacy of mid-century design that ranged from semi-serious clay sculpture to high camp gilded production pottery. His work can be seen in museum collections such as the Everson Museum of Art, Los Angeles County Museum of Art, Metropolitan Museum of Art, Cranbrook Academy, Guggenheim Museum of Art, Houston Museum of Art, and the Sculpture Center in New York. Of particular interest to collectors, pieces of Sascha Brastoff pottery (and enamels) frequently turn up at flea markets, antique shows, and shops.

Whether a lamp or an ashtray, Sascha Brastoff pottery can be readily recognized. Themes include prancing horses; roosters and exotic birds; dancers and other figures in exotic costumes; houses and rooftops, fruit, fish, and other animals such as walruses; and abstract geometric patterns, especially horizontal stripes. Color schemes tend toward grays, muted earthtones, deep teal, brown, navy blue, black, and white, with metallic gold generously applied as accents. Most finishes are extreme—either a very flat matte or a high gloss. Production pieces used more than sixty standard shapes, but Brastoff's special commissions and other studio pieces had no limits.

Signatures and marks are helpful for dating and identifying most pieces:

From 1940 until 1962 studio pieces executed by Brastoff were usually signed SASCHA BRASTOFF (with or without a date).

From 1947 to 1953 the signature SASCHA B. was handpainted on the front of the design, usually at the bottom, like a painting. These were painted by his staff.

Beginning in November 1953 the rooster logo was used as a backstamp in addition to the SASCHA B. signature on the front.

In the early 1960s after Brastoff left the company, a handwritten ® and a style number was added to the SASCHA B. signature (with or without the rooster backstamp). This was used until production ended in 1974, and although early designs were used, these pieces were made without Brastoff's input or supervision.

2.3 Detail of Rooftops.

2.1 Rooftops pattern with black background: vase, 9 1/2" height; pipe 4 1/2" height. 60-80; 40-50

2.2 Freeform dish/ashtray in same Rooftops pattern, 8 1/2" length. 40-50

2.4 Detail of Rooftops.

2.5 Rooftops pattern: F3 freeform plates, 9 3/4", with rooster backstamps. 50-60 each

2.6 Rooftops F1 freeform ashtrays, 7 1/4", with rooster backstamps. 35-45 each

2.7 Rooftops: left, F4 ashtray, 8 1/2"; center, O76 mug, 4 1/2" height; right, F2 ashtray, 11", with rooster backstamps. 40-60; 40-60; 55-70

2.8 Rooftops freeform ashtrays: left, F3 on light background, 9 1/2"; right, F6 on black background, 12 1/2", with rooster backstamps. 50-60; 70-90

Above:
2.9 Rooftops: left, C45 tea canister, 10 1/2" height; right, F21 canoe-shaped bowl, 7 1/4" length, with rooster backstamps. 150-200; 80-100

2.10 Rooftops: left, O6 8-inch square plate; center, F42 rounded plate, 10 1/2"; right, O3 6 1/4-inch square plate, with rooster backstamps. 40-50; 50-70; 30-40

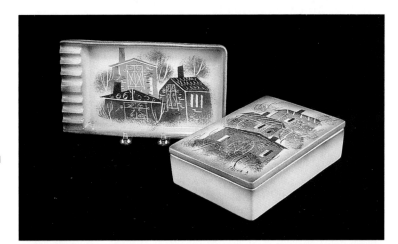

2.11 Rooftops: left, O5 slotted ashtray, 8 1/2"; right, O21 covered box, 7 5/8", with rooster backstamps (on lid of box). 60-80; 90-110

2.12 Rooftops: left, O44B large egg missing lid, 6 3/4" height; right, smaller O44A egg with lid, height 7 1/4", with rooster backstamps. 55-65; 75-95

Below:
2.13 Rooftops O53 charger with pastel colored houses, 17 1/4" diameter, with rooster backstamp. 250-350

2.14 Pagodas "cigar lovers" freeform oblong F8 ashtray, 17 1/2" length, with rooster backstamp. 200-300

2.15 Pagodas pattern on 17" O53 charger with rooster backstamp. 250-350

2.16 Pagodas: left, F2 freeform ashtray, 8 1/4"; right F6 large ashtray, 12 3/4", with rooster backstamps. 55-70; 70-90

2.17 Pagodas: bottom, O80 pipe, 4 1/2"; top, F44 bowl, 12 3/4", with rooster backstamps. 40-55; 85-110

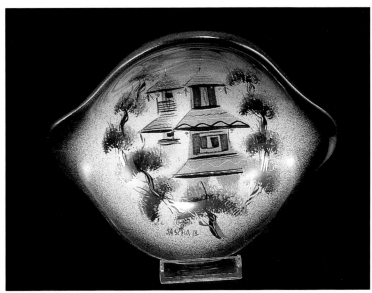

2.18 Pagodas C2 bowl, 7 1/4" across. 50-60

2.19 Freeform F44 bowl in matte finish with abstract design, 13", with rooster backstamp. 100-125

2.20 Detail of abstract design.

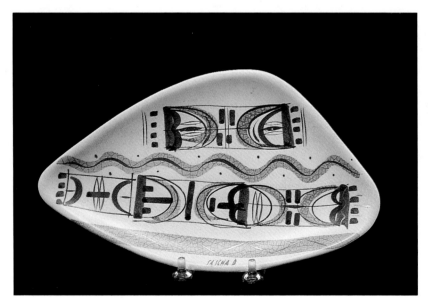

2.21 Freeform F3 plate with abstract totem design on white matte finish, 9 3/4", with rooster backstamp. 60-75

2.22 Detail of totem.

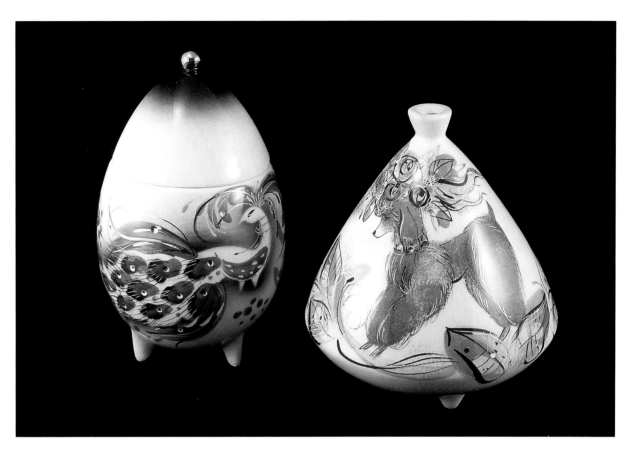

2.23 Left, O44A covered egg with Jewel Bird pattern, 7 1/2" height; right, H6 footed hooded ashtray with poodle motif, 7", with rooster backstamps. 70-90; 50-65

2.24 Left, M66 vase with pre-Columbian "Mayan" mosaic mask, 6" with rooster backstamp; right, More Gold 181 8-inch vase without rooster; center, M20 mosaic dish with fish, 5 1/2", no rooster. 100-125; 70-90; 25-35

2.25 Detail.

2.26 Left, O3 plate with
Aztec-Mayan metallic mask
6 1/2"; right, C30 ashtray in
blue, green, and gold,
10 1/4", no rooster
backstamps. 40-50; 50-60

2.27 Left, J10 orange
abstract design on
black triangular
ashtray, 7 3/4", no
rooster; center, 8-inch
square plate with bird
motif, no rooster; right,
O56 Vanity Fair with
pastel flowers, 7", with
rooster backstamp.
35-45; 40-60; 40-60

2.28 Left, Holiday Greetings
brown jug, 7 1/4"; right, O70
mug in Rooftops pattern,
5" height, rooster backstamp.
75-95; 35-45

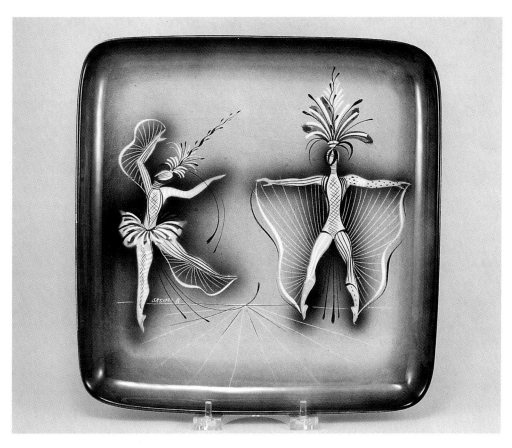

2.29 Square platter with ballet dancers, 14 3/4", no rooster. *Courtesy of Arthur and Ruth Marcus.* 150-200

2.31 Brastoff look-alike made by California Originals, 9" length, signed ANNE on front. *Courtesy of Merv and Sylvia Glickman.* 20-30

2.30 Detail of ballerina.

2.32 Surf Ballet footed bowls in yellow gold with applied gold swirls, part of dinnerware set, signed SASCHA B. on the back, 5 1/2" diameter. 25-35 each

2.33 Early dinnerware pattern, Smoke Tree, with white cotton-puff trees on a grey ground, introduced about 1949 and signed on front SASCHA B, 10, 8, and 6 1/2" diameters. *Courtesy of Elinor Polster.* 15-30 each

2.34 Smoke Tree pattern: punch bowl, 6 1/2" height, 14" diameter; shallow and deeper bowls, each 5 1/2" diameter. *Courtesy of Elinor Polster.* 200-250; 25-35 each

2.35 View of punch bowl showing scalloped rim.

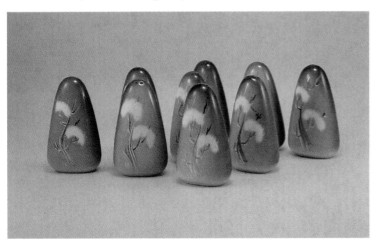

2.36 Salt and pepper shakers with grey and white Smoke Tree pattern. 4" height. *Courtesy of Elinor Polster.* 30-40 pair

2.37 Cup and saucer with Smoke Tree pattern. *Courtesy of Elinor Polster.*

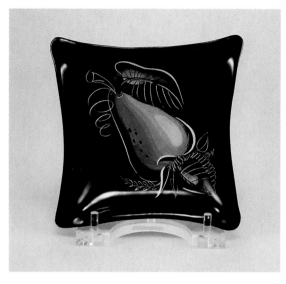

Above left:
2.38 Square ashtrays/shallow bowls with pulled corners, mustard yellow high gloss finish with fruit motifs, signed SASCHA B. on front, no rooster backstamp, 6 1/4" *Courtesy of Elinor Polster.* 30-40 each

Above right:
2.39 Square ashtray with purple eggplant, 6 1/4", no rooster. *Courtesy of Arthur and Ruth Marcus.* 35-45

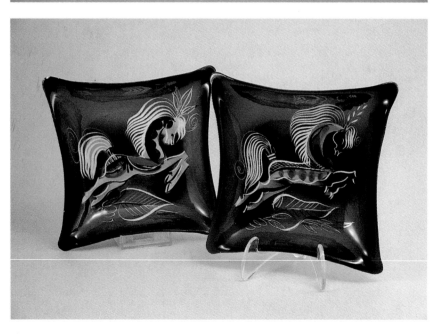

2.40 Ashtrays/shallow bowls in high gloss white with dark green rims and purple fruit motifs, signed SASCHA B. on front, no rooster backstamp, 6 1/4 " *Courtesy of Elinor Polster.* 35-45

2.41 Ashtrays/shallow bowls in high gloss grey with Star Steed prancing horse motif, signed SASCHA B. on front, no rooster backstamp, 6 1/4" square. *Courtesy of Elinor Polster.* 35-45

2.42 Ashtray/shallow bowl in high gloss white with pear motif, signed SASCHA B. on front, no rooster backstamp, 6 1/4" square. 30-40

2.43 Ashtray/shallow bowl in high gloss brown with fruit motif, signed SASCHA B. on front, no rooster backstamp, 7 3/4" square. 40-50

2.44 Detail.

2.45 Vase with cherry motif on yellow ground, high gloss, signed SASCHA B. on front, no rooster backstamp, 5 1/4" height. 60-70

2.46 Detail of cherry.

2.47 White ashtray/shallow bowl with blue poodle and pink and blue leaves, high gloss. 7" square. *Courtesy of Suite Lorain.* 40-50

2.48 Persian pattern with soft greys, matte finish, and gold accents: left, small rectangular ashtray, 4 1/4 " length; center, round ashtray, 7 1/8" diameter; right, square ashtray, 4 1/4", each signed on front and with rooster backstamp. 20-40 each

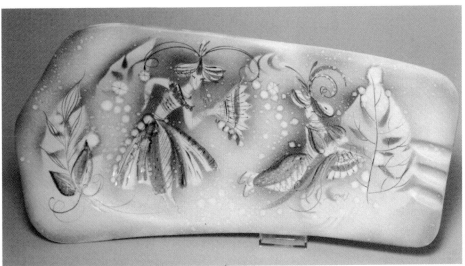

2.49 Large freeform F8 ashtray in Persian pattern, signed SASCHA B. on front with rooster backstamp, 17 5/8" length. 150-200

2.50 Freeform bowl in Misty Blue with abstract design in soft neutrals, 7 1/4" length. 30-40

134

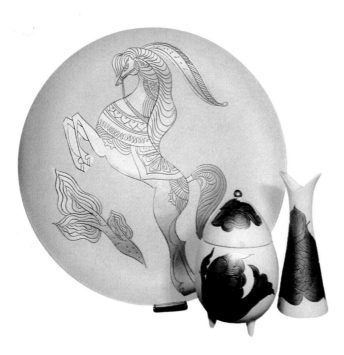

2.51 Aztec-Mayan in white bisque with sgraffito and metallic design, a late pattern introduced just before Sascha retired from the pottery: round chop plate or serving tray with prancing horse motif, 16 1/2" diameter; O44A covered egg on three legs with bird motif, signed SASCHA B. ® and rooster backstamp, indicating it was produced later and without Sascha. 7 1/2" height.; vase with double lip and metallic flower motif, also signed SASCHA B. ®. 8 in height. 200-250; 60-80; 45-55

2.52 Detail.

2.53 Egg-shaped O44A vase in Abstract Originals stripes pattern, 8" height, with rooster backstamp. 60-75

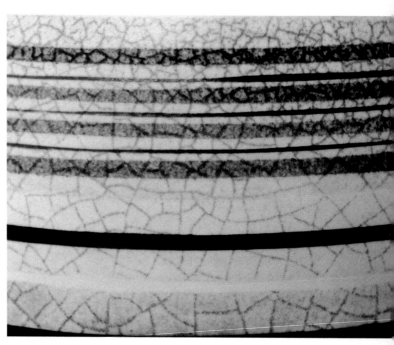

2.54 Detail of Stripes.

2.55 Enamel on copper plate in purple with white prancing horse, signed SASCHA B, 11 3/4" diameter. 75-100

2.56 Enamel on copper ashtray in dull green, black, and ochre houses (Rooftops) pattern, 10" diameter. 60-80

2.57 Detail of houses.

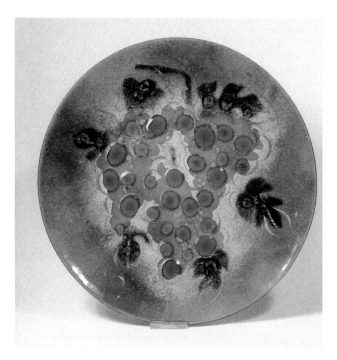

2.58 Enamel on copper plate in dull green with orange and green grapes, signed SASCHA B, 11 3/4" diameter. 75-95

2.59 Enamel on copper plate in red-orange with applied gold glass blobs, signed SASCHA B, 11 3/4" diameter. 75-95

2.60 Enamel on copper plate in turquoise with blue and green grapes, signed SASCHA B, 11 3/4 in diameter. 75-95

2.61 Enamel on copper ashtray in olive green with blue and white flowers, signed SASCHA B, 6 1/4" diameter. 30-40

2.63 Enamel on copper footed vase in dull green with applied glass grapes, signed SASCHA B, 7" height. 65-85

2.62 Enamel on copper compote in dark green with floral decoration, signed SASCHA B, 11" diameter, 4" height. 65-85

2.64 Small enamel on copper plate with plant on rust background, 4" diameter. 10-20

2.65 Left, enamel on copper bowl in purple with bird motif, 6 7/8"; right, enamel on copper vase with Rooftops pattern, 5" height. 60-75; 30-40

2.67 Enamel on copper cigarette holder/vases with flower motif. 15-20 each

2.66 Left, enamel on copper 8" orange ashtray with red maple leaves; right, 8" ashtray in green with flowers. 60-75 each

2.68 Resin sculpture of Tiki or native mask in dark chartreuse, 10 1/4" height. 100-125

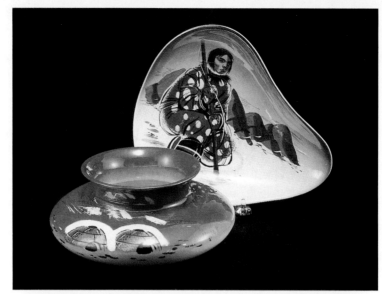

2.69 Left, O91 four-legged planter with igloo on dark red-orange, 7 1/2" height; right, F40 freeform plate with Eskimo in spotted fur coat, 9 1/2" length. 85-110; 65-95

Alaska series by Matthew Adams

Matthew Adams designed the Alaska series which was decorated with motifs of Eskimos and their land and culture. The following examples do not have a rooster backstamp but are signed on the front with the usual SASCHA B.

2.70 Detail of Eskimo.

2.71 Left, S52 shell-shaped plate with totem, 4 3/4" height; right, C14 three-legged fish-shaped footed bowl with log cabin, 9 1/2" length. 95-115 each

2.72 Left, H6 high hooded ashtray with Eskimo, 7" height; bottom right, CB23 box with Eskimo, 5 1/2"; top center, R13 plate with Eskimo, 12 1/2". 100-125 each

2.73 Detail of box.

2.74 O54 seven-compartment tray with female Eskimo, 14 1/2" length. 150-175

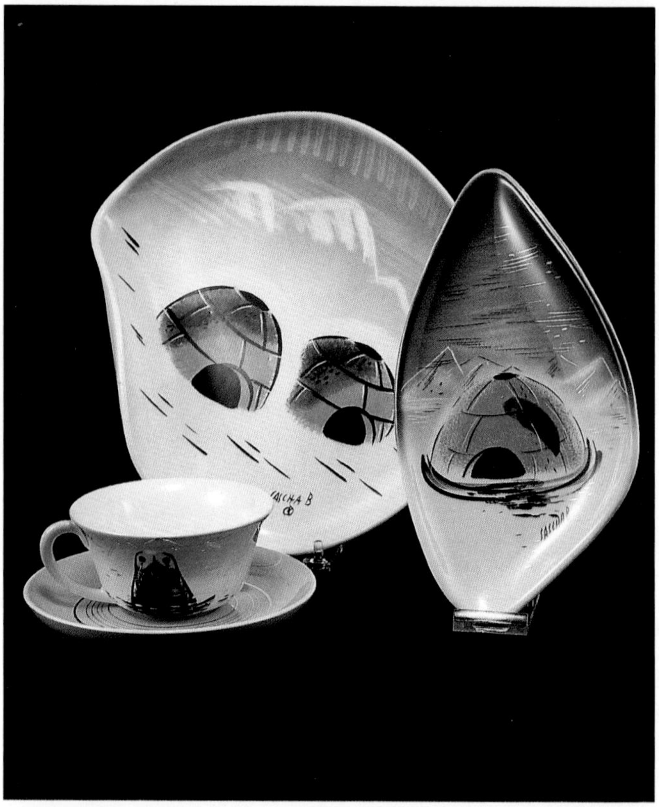

2.76 Left, cup and saucer with seal motif on blue, 6 1/2" height; center, plate with blue igloo on grey, 10 1/2"; right, F3 freeform plate with blue igloo on blue and grey, 9 3/4" length. 40-60; 60-80; 55-70

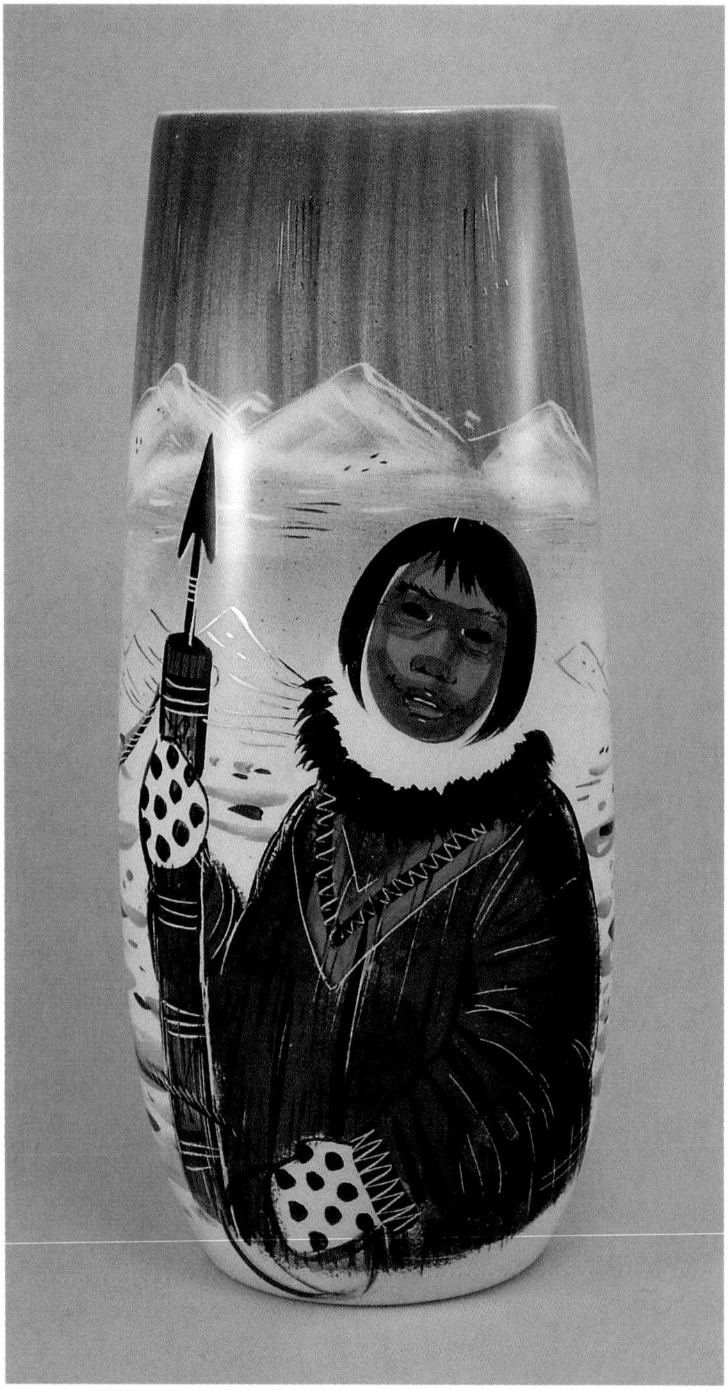

2.75 Dull green vase with Eskimo and harpoon, 12 1/8" height. 175-225

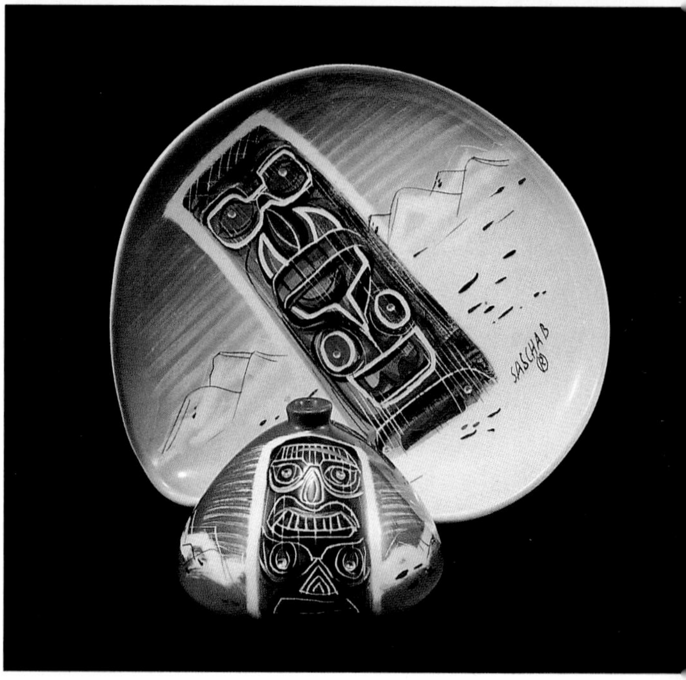

2.77 Top, F42 grey-green plate with totem, 11"; bottom, H3 hooded ashtray with totem, 4 1/4" height. 70-90; 50-70

2.78 E13 blue and white bowl with elk, 12 1/2" diameter. 85-135

2.79 F40 freeform bowl with Eskimo on green, 10" length. 80-100

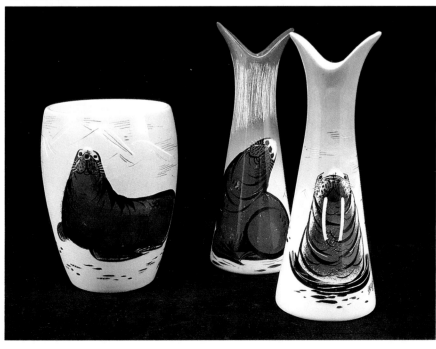

2.80 Left, F20 round vase with brown seal, 5 1/2" height; O82 split lip 8" vases, each with brown walrus. 80-100; 60-80

2.81 Left, A301 bud vase with walrus on yellow ground, 7 3/4" height; center, F2 freeform ashtray with walrus on grey, 8 1/2"; right, O81 split lip vase with seal on dark blue, 5 1/2" height. 65-75 each

2.82 Left, O11 4-inch salt and pepper shakers with blue igloos on green; center, O68 10 1/2" pitcher with Eskimo on blue; right O82 8" split lip vase with blue igloo. 40-50 pair; 150-170; 60-80

2.83 Left, H3 low hooded ashtray with polar bear on blue, 4 1/4 in; center, F4 7" bowl with totem on blue ground, with inscription GIFT FROM BETA CHAPTER FAIRBANKS, AK; right, H6 high hooded ashtray with polar bear on blue, 7" height. 55-75; 45-65; 75-95

Matthew Adams

After working for Sascha Brastoff and introducing the popular Alaska pattern, Adams left and made similar pottery in his own studio. The following examples of Alaska are signed MATTHEW ADAMS.

2.84 Left, yellow salt and pepper shakers with moose, 3 3/4"; right, yellow salt and pepper shakers with igloo and dog sled, 3 3/4" height. 35-45 pair

2.85 Top, yellow 161 plate with Eskimo girl, 11 1/2"; bottom, round yellow 143B vase with seal, 4 1/2" height. 85-115; 60-75

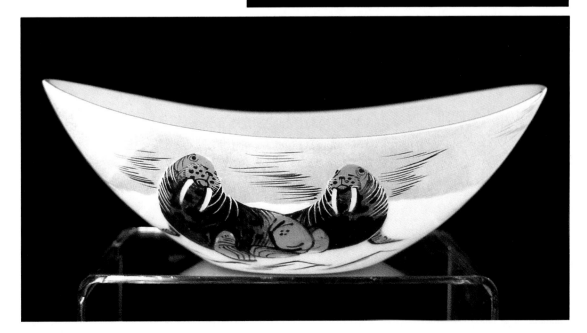

2.86 Blue 136 canoe-shaped bowl with walrus, 14 3/4" length. 100-125

2.87 Left, glacier 190A bowl, 8 3/4"; right, blue 161 plate with Eskimo throwing harpoon, 11 1/2". 60-75; 85-115

2.88 Left, blue tray with cabin on stilts, 7 3/4"; right center, 115A blue 10-inch vase with cabin on stilts; left center and right, salt and pepper shakers with iceberg, 4" height. 50-60; 80-100; 40-50 pair

2.89 Center, 182A dull green teapot with walrus, 7 1/4"; matching salt and pepper shakers with walrus, 5" height. 125-145; 60-75 pair

2.90 Left, blue 181A 6" pitcher with ram; center, blue O99B bowl with seal, 7 1/2" marked ALASKA; right, cup with polar bear. 70-90; 50-60; 25-35

2.91 Left, 195 blue 9" three-legged vase with Eskimo children; right, blue 158 7" covered candy box with walrus. 90-110; 115-135

2.92 Left, 162 green 7 1/2" plate with igloo and sled; center, 190B green bowl with Eskimo child, 9 3/4"; right, 183B vase with totem pole, 4 1/4" height. 40-60; 80-100; 40-60

2.93 Detail.

Right:
2.94 176 spoon rest with mountain and glacier motif, 9 5/8" marked ALASKA. 40-60

2.95 Left, O83 three-legged 5" hooded ashtray with polar bear; center, 083 hooded ashtray with husky; right, blue hooded ashtray with ashtray/lighter combination with polar bear, 5 1/4" height. 40-60; 40-60; 75-95

2.96 Left, blue bowl with seal, 9 1/4"; right, three-legged 138 blue bowl with walrus, 6 1/4" height. 75-95; 50-60

2.97 Left, 185A blue ashtray with polar bear, 7"; right, 183A lighter with husky, 5 1/2" height. 50-60 each

Chapter Three:
Marc Bellaire

Marc Bellaire, originally Donald Edmund Fleischman, (1925-1994) was born in Toledo, Ohio, the son of Fredrick Francis Fleischman and Edna Octavia (Bellaire) Fleischman. He began to take classes at the Toledo Museum of Art at an early age, and as a teenager, he studied under American watercolorist Ernest Spring. While at Macomber High School, he did some designing for the Libbey Glass Co. After serving in the United States Navy in World War II and touring the South Pacific and Orient, he studied art at Wayne University in Detroit, the American Academy of Art in Chicago, and at the Chicago Art Institute.

The West Coast attracted Bellaire, so in 1950 he studied at the Art Institute in Los Angeles. Although primarily a painter and sculptor, Bellaire designed and produced his own line of hand-decorated pottery. After building a 10,000 square foot studio in Culver City, California, he was able to produce for a national market. Bellaire's particular style of California Fifties pottery is remarkably similar to that of Sascha Brastoff. It is not clear whether he developed the style while working at the Brastoff plant or that he worked for Brastoff because of his style. In either case, there was no denying its popularity, and Bellaire also became involved in other projects such as effects for Hollywood films as well as for Disneyland and for Las Vegas night clubs in the early 1950s. The years 1951 to 1956 were especially fruitful, and Bellaire was named by *Giftware* magazine as one of the top ten designers of artware. In addition to his own studio production, his designs included a line of lamps for the Rembrandt Lamp Co. in Chicago and glassware for a New York based company. He operated a studio and an art gallery in Crittenden, Virginia in the 1960s.

After 1956, Bellaire began to devote more of his time to teaching, lecturing, and writing on art, design, and ceramic decorating in the United States and Canada. His books included *Underglaze Decoration* and *Brush Decoration*, and he wrote regularly for periodicals such as *Ceramic Monthly* and *Popular Ceramics*. The opening remarks in one of his how-to books summed up his approach to creative decorating: "Learn to see....look at things around you individually—not collectively as you would if you were looking through a window. Pick up a leaf, a twig, or a piece of fruit and study its basic shape....try to find the symbol of the object you wish to represent..." (Bellaire Underglaze 3)

Bellaire's formula method of decorating ceramics was used to make textured backgrounds and a range of motifs that included fruit, birds, animals, and figures—especially stylized beachcombers, harlequins, and exotic native dancers. His lessons on technique included a word of advice—to look at artistic expression as fun. Without the element of pleasure and relaxation, there was no purpose in practicing ceramic decorating or other form of art, according to Bellaire. His flamboyant Fifties pottery is a testament to this philosophy.

In addition to his success in ceramics, Bellaire was an accomplished painter, muralist, and sculptor; his work was exhibited in the United States and Mexico and is found in important collections and country clubs from California to Florida. From 1982 his studio was located at 33669 Date Palm, Drive in Cathedral City, California. He died in 1994.

3.1 Mardi Gras pillow vase in black, white, grey, vivid pink, and turquoise, 7 1/4 x 8 3/4". 250-325

3.2 Mardi Gras eight-slot ashtray, 14 1/2" diameter. 275-350

3.3 Mardi Gras: left, three-slot ashtray, 10" diameter; right, two-slot oblong ashtray, 6 1/2" diameter. 140-165; 45-65

3.4 Mardi Gras: left, coaster, 4 5/8" diameter; right, three-slot ashtray, 8 1/2" length. 45-55; 90-120

3.5 Mardi Gras: top left, two-slot oblong ashtray, 6 1/2" length; center, bottom right and left, two three-slot ashtrays, 4 1/2" each; center, covered freeform box, 8" length. 60-75; 40-60; 175-225

3.6 Mardi Gras covered boxes: left, 5" height; right, 9" diameter. 165-195; 250-295

3.7 Detail of Mardi Gras.

3.8 Mardi Gras charger with light background, 14" diameter, signed "Especially designed for Madeline." 250-295

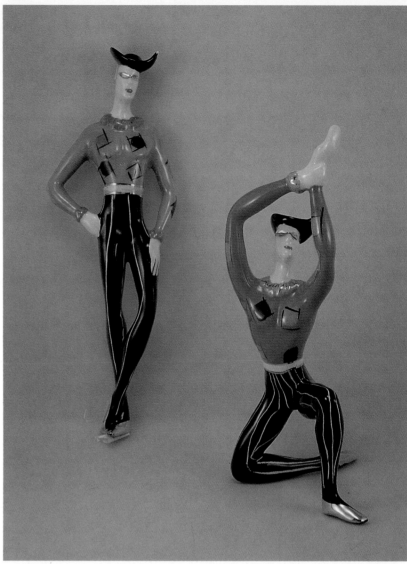

3.9 Mardi Gras figurines: left, standing, 11 1/4" height; right, half kneeling, 10" height. 375-425 each

Below:
3.10 Jamaica musician figurines: left, guitar player, 6 3/8 height; center, horn player, 9" height; right, bongo player, 8 1/2" height. 600-675 each

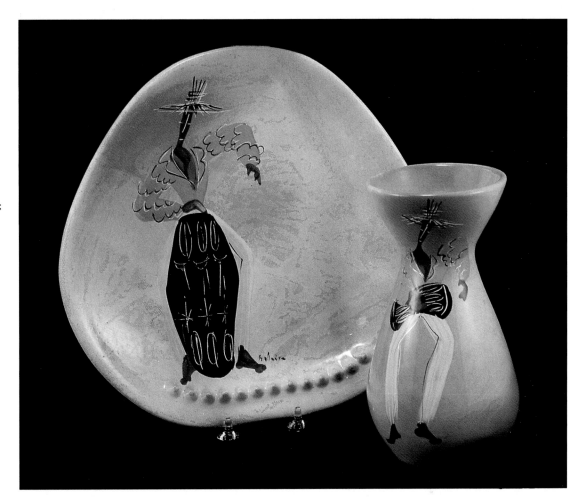

3.11 Jamaica: left, 12" plate; right, 8" vase. 120-140 each

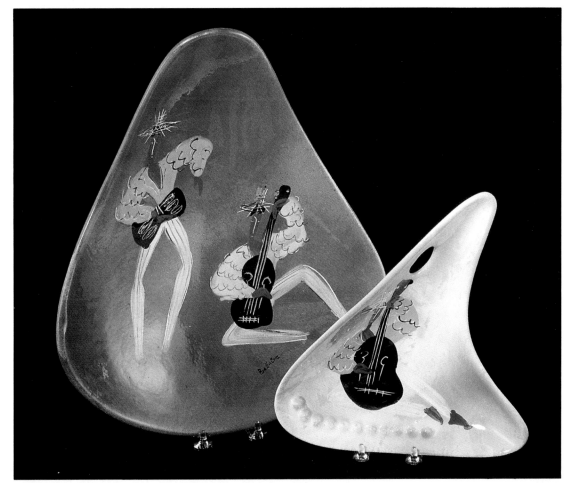

3.12 Jamaica: left, freeform shallow bowl, 15" length; right, boomerang ashtray, 11 1/2" length. 175-225; 90-110

3.13 Balinese pattern with
dancers on pinkish background:
center, pillow vase, 7 1/4"
height; left and right,
candleholders, 7 3/4" height.
225-275; 225-275 pair

3.14 Balinese oblong ashtray,
10" length. 80-100

3.15 Balinese: left, coaster,
4 3/4" diameter; right,
triangular ashtray, 6" length.
30-50; 95-115

3.16 Detail of Balinese.

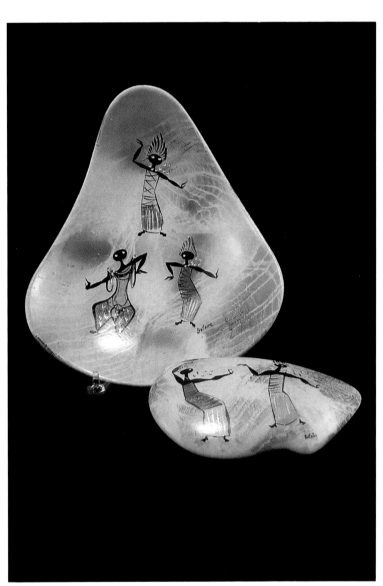

3.17 Top, Balinese shallow bowl, 12 1/2" Diameter; bottom, covered box, 8" length. 150-175; 175-200

Left:
3.18 Beachcomber cocktail mixer in white coated glass, 9 1/4" height. 30-50

Above:
3.20 Beachcomber bowl, 6 1/2" diameter.
100-125

3.19 Beachcomber bowl, 12 1/2" diameter.
175-200

3.21 Friendly Island on mottled earth toned background: left, round bowl, 9 1/8"; right, freeform, 9 3/8" length. 95-115; 75-95

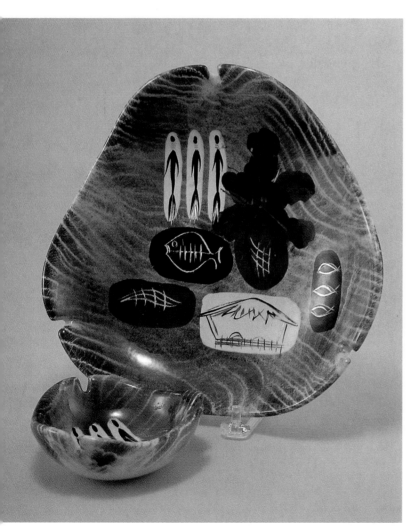

3.22 Friendly Island: bottom, three-slot ashtray bowl, 4 1/8"; top, three-slot ashtray plate, 9" diameter. 25-35; 75-95

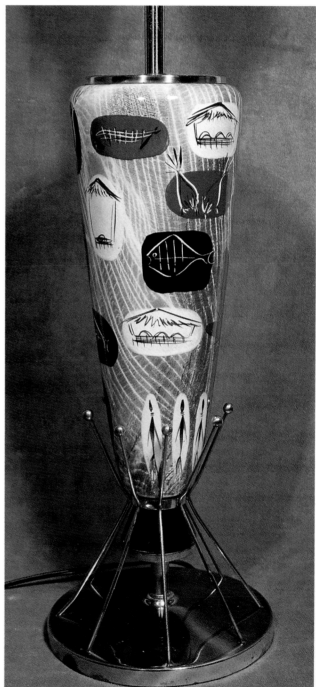

3.23 Friendly Island lamp base, ceramic portion 12 1/2" height. 200-250

Right:
3.25 Yellow vase/lamp base with deep orange and black reserves decorated with stick figures, 14" height. 115-135

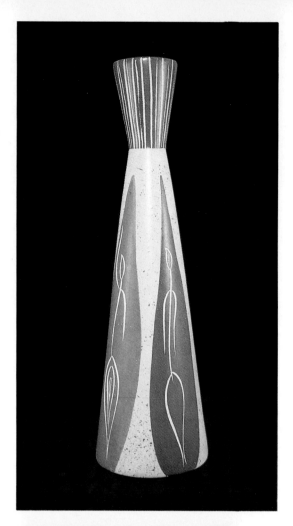

3.24 Lamp base with donkey, antelope, and wild boar, ceramic portion 18 1/4" height. 225-295

Right:
3.26 Decanter with lid and handle decorated with classical figures in pink and purple togas on a white ground, 13" height. 300-350

3.27 Footed vase with Oriental motifs on white bisque, 9 1/2" height.
250-300

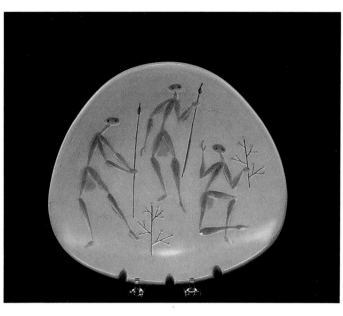

3.29 Spear throwers ashtray, 9 3/4" length. 125-150

3.28 Detail of tree.

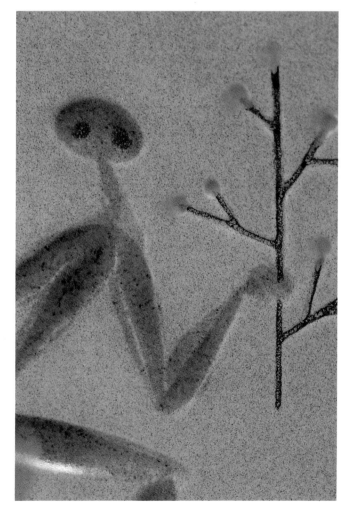

3.30 Detail of figure.

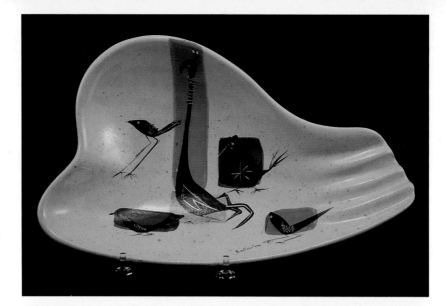

3.31 Bird Isle freeform ashtray,
15 1/5" length. 135-165

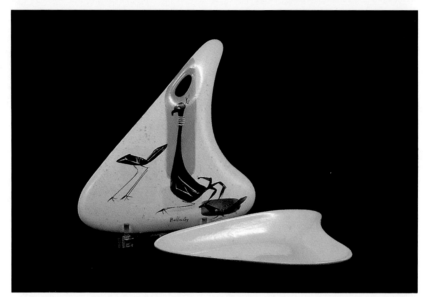

3.32 Bird Isle freeform covered
box, 11 1/2" long side. 175-225

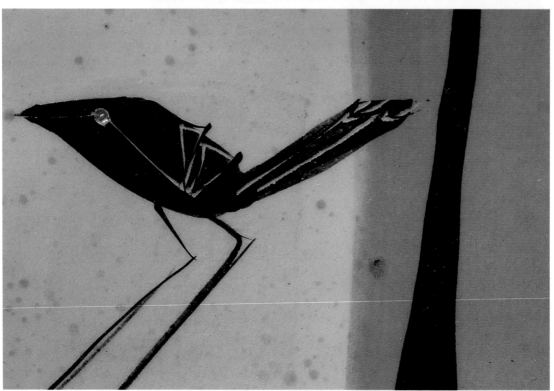

3.33 Detail of bird.

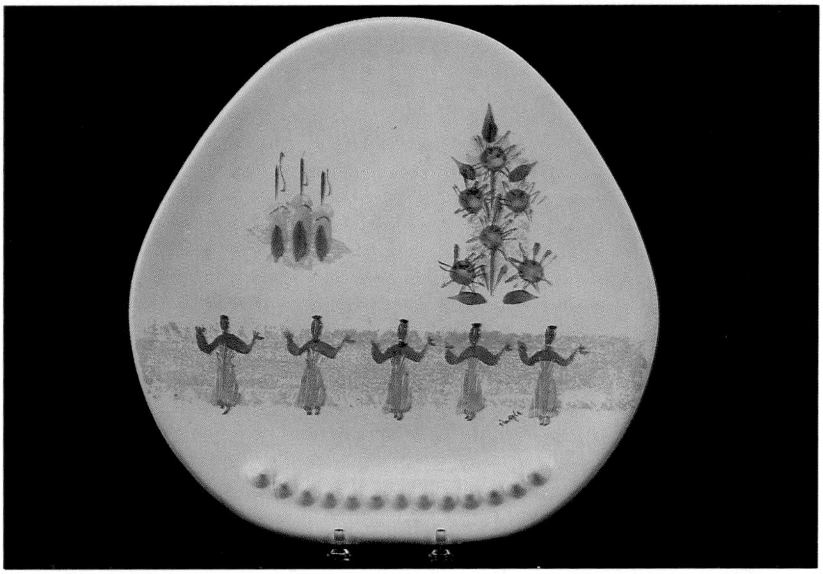

3.34 Kashmir ashtray, 12" length. 75-100

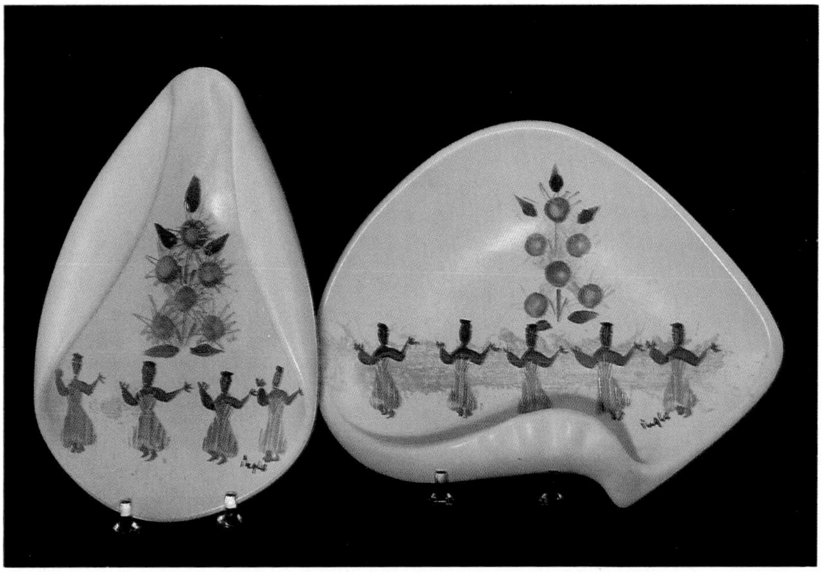

3.35 Kashmir: left, double-fold freeform ashtray, 8 1/2" length; right, single-fold freeform ashtray, 9 1/2" length.. 100-120; 120-140

Below:
3.36 Kashmir freeform boomerang box with cover, 11 1/2" length, signed INGLE on the front. 165-195

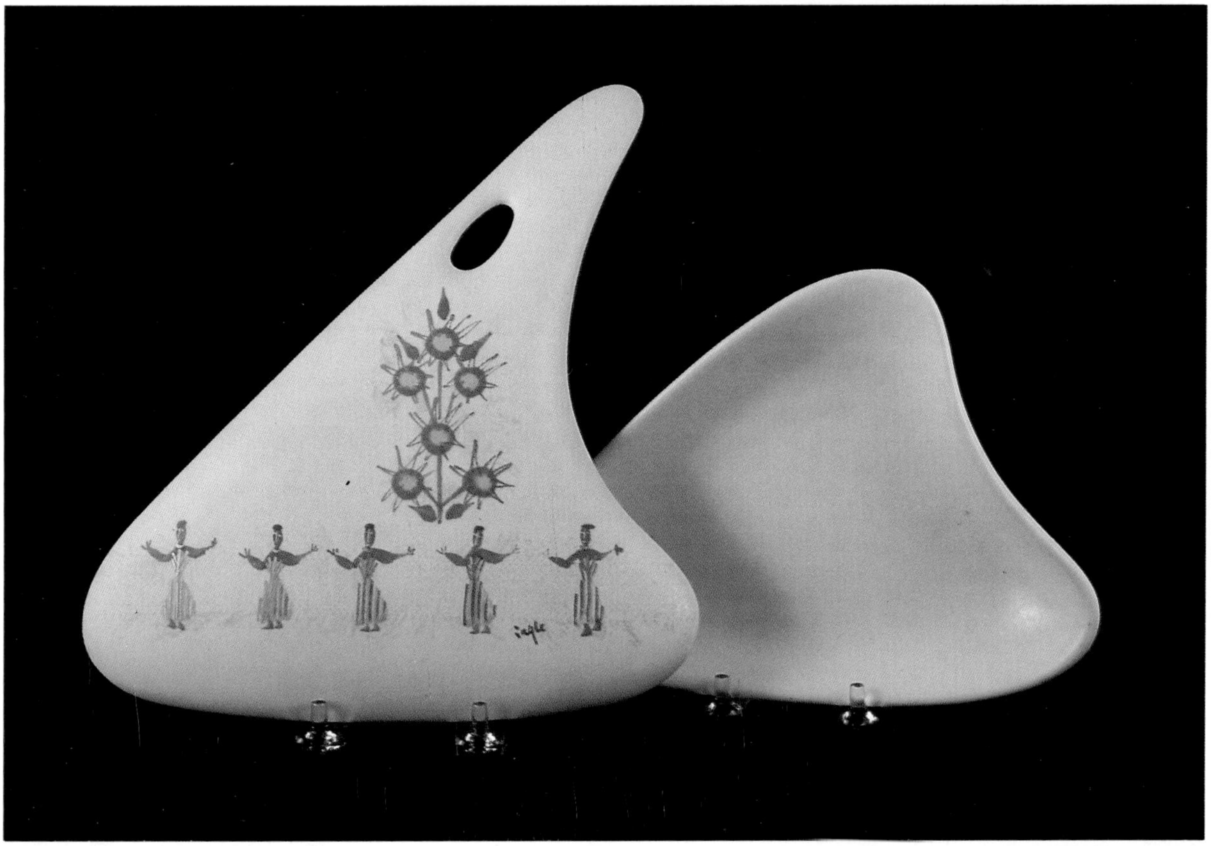

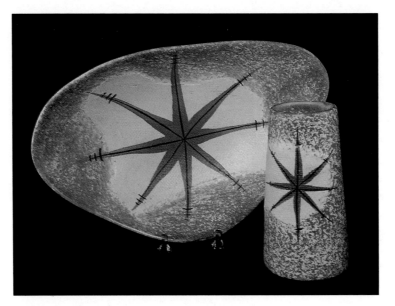

3.37 Polynesian Star with burlap texture: left, freeform plate, 12 1/2" length; right, vase, 6" height. 60-75; 40-50

3.38 Polynesian Star: left, square bottle vase, 7 1/2" height; right, decanter with lid, 13" height. 150-175; 125-150

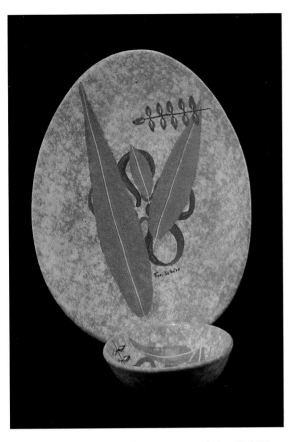

3.39 Luau with grey leaves decoration: top, oval plate, 10 1/2";
bottom, round bowl, 4 1/2" diameter. 50-70; 20-25

3.40 Still Life with fruit in pink and muted tones: small 5" square plate and large 11" round plate.
25-35; 60-80

3.41 Hawaiian figures on pink mottled ground: left, ashtray, 5 3/4"; right, lamp base, 7 1/2" square. 60-80; 200-250

3.42 Oriental with colorfully dressed figures holding parasols: left, shallow bowl, 9 1/2"; right, freeform ashtray, 12 1/2" length. 80-100; 100-150

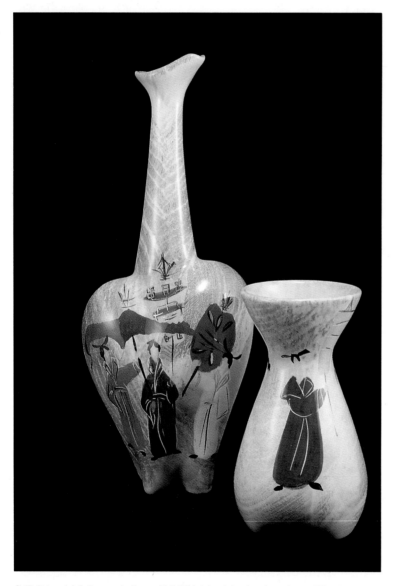

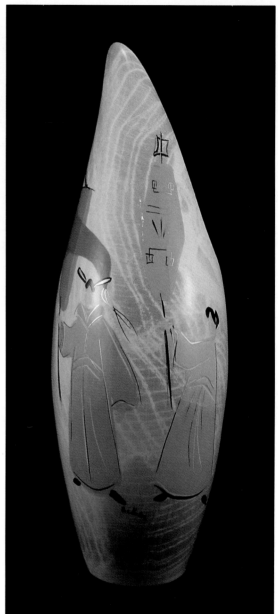

3.44 Oriental freeform vase, 15 1/2" height. 225-275

3.43 Oriental: left, long-necked vase, 15 3/4" height; right, three-legged vase, 8" height. 250-275; 100-125

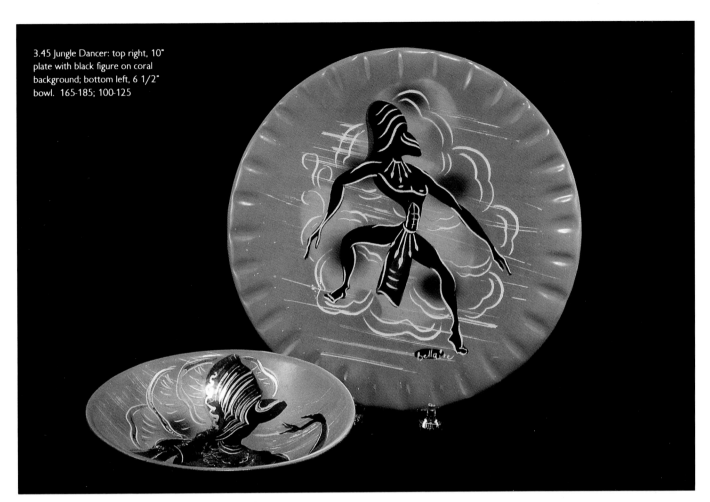

3.45 Jungle Dancer: top right, 10"
plate with black figure on coral
background; bottom left, 6 1/2"
bowl. 165-185; 100-125

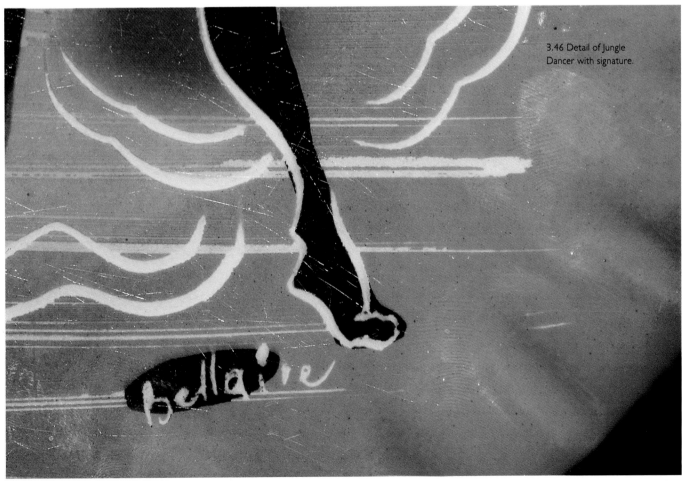

3.46 Detail of Jungle
Dancer with signature.

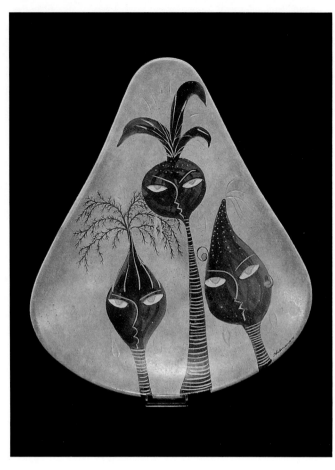

3.47 Black onion heads on pink freeform plate, 15 1/2" length, front with signature "Halmarian," back incised MARC BELLAIRE © 1959. 250-275

3.49 Four-lobed amoeboid bowl with native dancer on light green ground, 12 3/8" length. 175-225

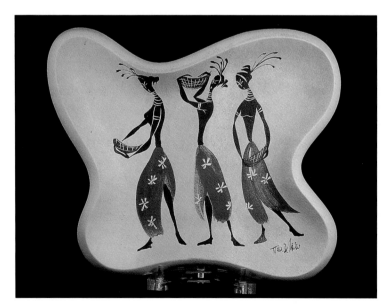

3.48 Four-lobed amoeboid bowl with native women in brown skirts, 14" across. 225-250

3.50 Lion motif on round scalloped plate, 12 1/2" diameter. 125-150

3.51 Dark green bowls decorated with brown and gold leaves: left, oval 10 1/4"; right, round, 6 1/2" diameter. 65-85; 50-60

3.53 Freeform bowl with linear faces on brown and black background, 11" length, additional signature on back VICKY MONRO ORIGINAL 1957 HOUSTON. 40-50

3.52 Bowl decorated with brown leaves radiating from the center, 6 3/4" diameter. 45-55

3.54 Freeform plate with orange abstraction on brown, 11" length, incised BELLAIRE RUBY. 30-40

Chapter Four:
Frances & Michael Higgins

"We offer you no polysyllabic mystique, nor any fervent analysis of our approach to our work. It is just what our lives steered us into doing for our joint living, and we like it most of the time."
—*Frances and Michael Higgins quoted in Fifty-50.*

While attending an American Ceramic Society conference in 1942, Frances Stewart first got the idea to work with glass. Without formal training in glassmaking, she and her husband Michael would work almost exclusively with new glassmaking techniques requiring neither large furnaces nor sophisticated equipment. They began experimenting with commercial plate and window glass. Cut to the outline of a mold, the glass would then sag into the contour of the mold when heated in a kiln. Sagging and bending flat glass and using decorating methods such as enameling, laminating, and gilding, the Higginses pioneered a new glass industry beginning in 1948.

Frances Stewart was born in Haddock, Georgia on December 24, 1912. She earned a Bachelor of Science degree at the Georgia State College for Women (Georgia College). While teaching junior high school in Atlanta from 1935 to 1944, she continued her education during the summers: 1936 at Columbia University Teachers College; 1940, 1941, and 1942 at Sophie Newcomb College studying pottery with Kenneth Smith; and 1944 at Ohio State University. From 1944 to 1948 she taught art at the University of Georgia, and again, studied during the summers. Beginning with the summer of 1946, she worked on a Master of Fine Arts degree at the Institute of Design in Chicago. She continued in 1947, and then won a Rockefeller Foundation Fellowship to complete the degree in 1948. In the meantime, she met Michael Higgins, who taught and then headed the Visual Design Department at the Institute of Design.

Michael Higgins was born in London on September 29, 1908. He studied at Eton College, King's College, Cambridge University, and at the London Central School of Arts and Crafts. After working in advertising art, he emigrated to the United States in 1938 and lived in New Orleans, Washington D. C., and then moved to Chicago in 1947, where he met Frances. They married in 1948 and began to experiment with fusing glass, beginning with clear glass and hand drawn decoration. In 1950 they decided to hire someone to help with glass cutting, so they could devote more time to designing and decorating the glass. They worked together in the studio throughout the 1950s until 1958 when Dearborn Glass, an industrial glass company outside Chicago, invited them to set up a studio. The original arrangement called for only a two day a week commitment at Dearborn so the couple could continue to work part of the time in their own studio. However, after beginning the Dearborn production, they realized that overseeing the operation demanded all of their attention.

The six years at Dearborn, from 1958 to 1964, were the years in which the largest quantity of Higgins' pieces were produced. Once the designs were created, the glass went through a kind of mass production. In order to sign each piece, a gold signature was screened on the front before sending it through the last heating. Engraving each signature would simply have been too time consuming. Both Frances and Michael developed new colors and enamels for the double-layered flat glass plates, bowls, and ashtrays made at Dearborn. Since each bore the gold screened signature, dating of these items is fairly simple. During this time they also experimented with techniques that were not used commercially such as weaving copper wire into the glass, fusing glass chips into crystalline forms, and overlaying colors and patterns onto glass panels.

When they left Dearborn in 1964, they took all of the newly developed colors with them. Haeger Pottery invited the Higginses to establish a glass studio at the pottery, so they brought their kiln, lehr, molds, and glazes and set up there. The gold signature was also used on the front of Haeger pieces, and they did some experimenting with mirrors, but only for about a year and a half. They left in 1966 and decided to work alone in their own studio. During the late 1960s and early 1970s they each made glass plaques, engraved either Michael or Frances on the fronts, and framed them in wood. Most of their work, however, bears the single-word signature "Higgins" because of their close collaboration with both ideas and execution. In 1972 the Higgins purchased a vacant building in Riverside, Illinois near Chicago and opened the studio that is still in operation today. Rather than a signature on the front, they returned to the earlier method of engraving one on the back of each piece. Since there are no successors, when Frances and Michael retire, Higgins glass will no longer be made. Museums with holdings of Higgins glass include the Victoria and Albert Museum, the Metropolitan Museum of Art, the Corning Museum of Glass, the American Craft Museum, and the Johnson Wax Collection.

4.1 Plaque with fish design in pastels, engraved signature on the front, MICHAEL HIGGINS 72, and one of the studio pieces designed by only Michael or Frances, rather than as a collaboration. 7 3/4 x 13 3/4" without frame. This is the same piece originally seen in Grover's *Contemporary Art Glass.* 1,000-1,200

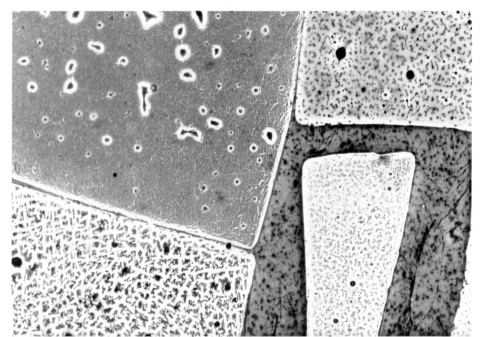

4.2 Detail of fish.

4.3 Detail of fish.

4.4 Abstract relief plaque with engraved signature on the front, FRANCES HIGGINS 71, also pictured in Grover. 6" x 9" without frame. 1,000-1,200

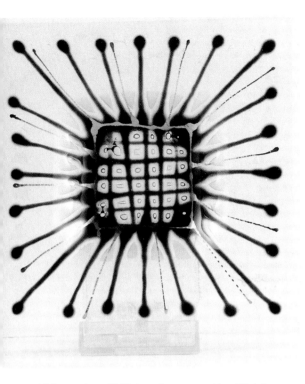

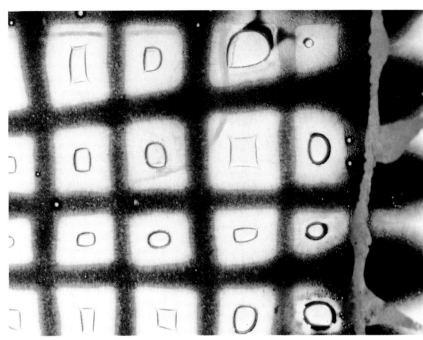

4.5 Square plate with black on clear center grid and black linear pattern radiating from the center. 60-70

4.6 Detail of grid.

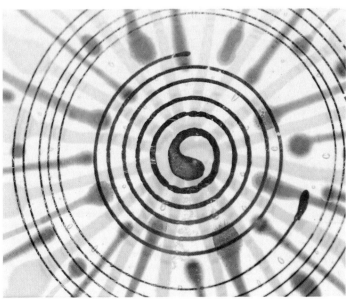

4.7 Small flat plates in clear glass with black bead on string pattern radiating from the center. 5" diameter, etched signature. *Courtesy of Studio Moderne.* 25-35 each

4.8 Detail.

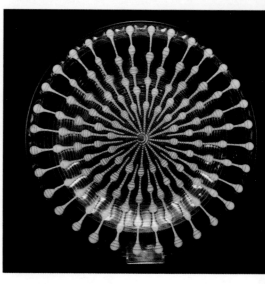

4.9 Bowl in clear glass with bead on string radiating pattern. 12" diameter, with Dearborn signature. *Courtesy of Donna and Rodney Wasserstrom.* 100-125

4.10 Flat plate in clear with white bead on string pattern. 12 1/4 " diameter, with Dearborn signature. *Courtesy of Donna and Rodney Wasserstrom.* 75-100

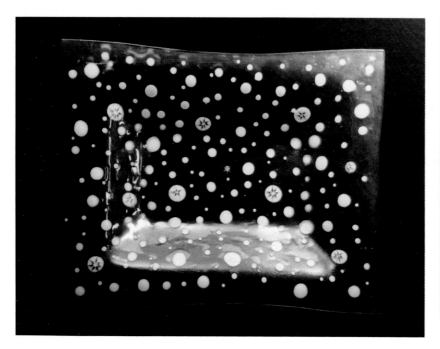

4.11 Clear rectangular plate decorated with white spots in varying sizes, etched signature. 15 3/4" length. *Courtesy of Studio Moderne.* 100-125

4.12 Detail of spots.

4.13 Rectangular plate with turquoise and white irregular rectangles, overlaid with gold. 14" length, with Dearborn signature. *Courtesy of Studio Moderne.* 80-110

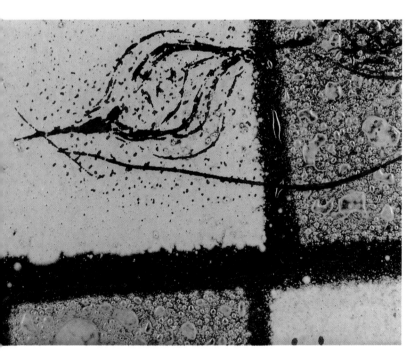

4.14 Detail of rectangles.

4.15 Freeform plate with white and turquoise geometric pattern overlaid with gold, with Dearborn signature. *Courtesy of Studio Moderne.* 70-90

4.16 Small square 4" ashtrays with central sun motif: two-tone yellow and two-tone orange, with Dearborn signatures. *Courtesy of Donna and Rodney Wasserstrom.* 25-35 each

4.17 Detail of orange.

4.18 Detail of yellow.

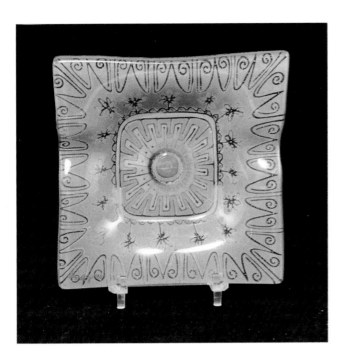

4.19 Small square 4" purple ashtray, with Dearborn signature. *Courtesy of Donna and Rodney Wasserstrom.* 25-35

4.21 Large squarish plate in turquoise with internal spiral decoration. 13 1/2 x 13 1/2" *Courtesy of Studio Moderne.* 90-110

4.20 Detail.

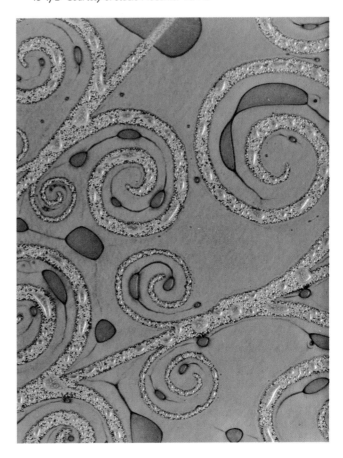

4.22 Detail of spiral.

178

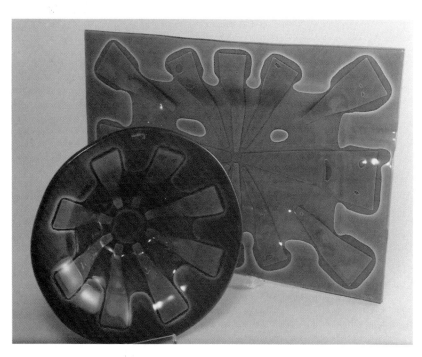

4.23 Orange on orange bowl, 8" diameter; and rectangular plate, 14 x 10", with Dearborn signatures. *Courtesy of Donna and Rodney Wasserstrom.* 75-95 each

4.25 Purple bowls with purple and brown triangular spokes radiating from the center. 12" and 8 1/4" diameters, with Dearborn signature. *Courtesy of Studio Moderne.* 90-110; 60-90

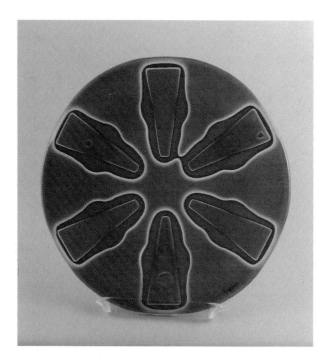

4.24 Orange plate with six-spoked wheel motif. 8 1/4" diameter, with Dearborn signature. *Courtesy of Donna and Rodney Wasserstrom.* 55-65

4.26 Purple with purple and brown rectangles: left, square plate, 7 x 7"; top, large round plate, 12 1/4" diameter; bottom, bowl, 8 1/8" diameter, with Dearborn signatures. *Courtesy of Donna and Rodney Wasserstrom.* 40-50; 80-90; 70-80

4.27 Left, rectangular clear plate with turquoise "beads on a string" radiating from the center, 10 x 5"; right, squarish turquoise plate with spiral decoration, 7 1/4" square, with Dearborn signatures. *Courtesy of Donna and Rodney Wasserstrom.* 50-60 each

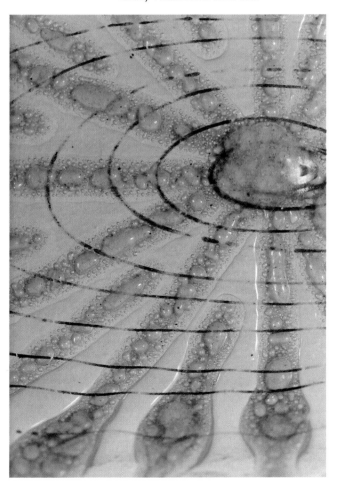

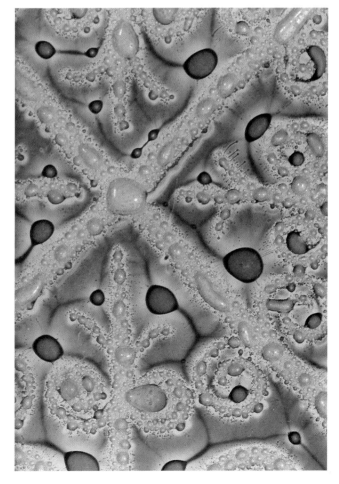

4.28 Detail of rectangular plate.

4.29 Detail of square plate.

4.30 Rectangular plate with earth tone abstract stripes resembling torn paper, overlaid with gold flower-like motif. 7 x 4 3/4", with Dearborn signature. *Courtesy of Donna and Rodney Wasserstrom.* 70-80

4.32 Freeform plate with yellow stripes radiating from the center, 13" longest side, with Dearborn signature. *Courtesy of Donna and Rodney Wasserstrom.* 90-110

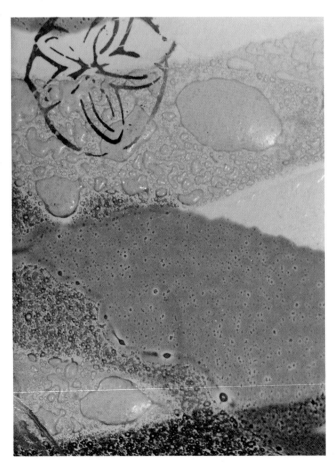

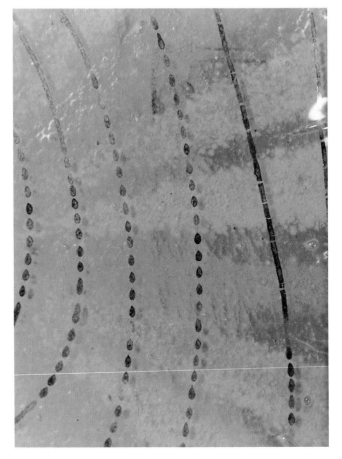

4.31 Detail of earth tone.

4.33 Detail of stripes.

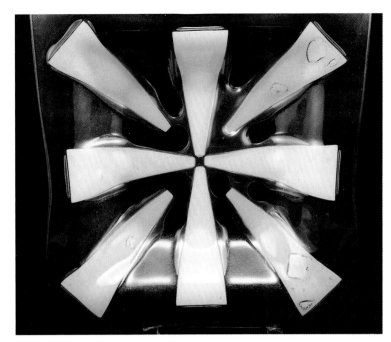

4.34 Square plate with triangles in shades of yellow-green. 9 5/8", with Dearborn signature. *Courtesy of Donna and Rodney Wasserstrom.* 60-80

4.35 Rectangular plates with flower motif: left, yellow-greens; right, oranges. 4 3/4 x 7", with Dearborn signatures. *Courtesy of Donna and Rodney Wasserstrom.* 40-50 each

4.36 Same plates with different lighting.

182

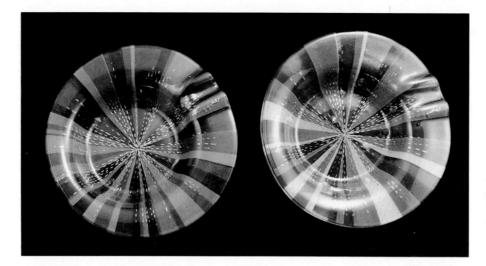

4.37 Roundish ashtrays with alternating color stripes: left, pink and blue; right, green and blue. 5 1/4 diameters, with Dearborn signatures. *Courtesy of Donna and Rodney Wasserstrom.* 30-40 each

4.38 Detail of pink and blue.

4.39 Detail of green and blue with signature.

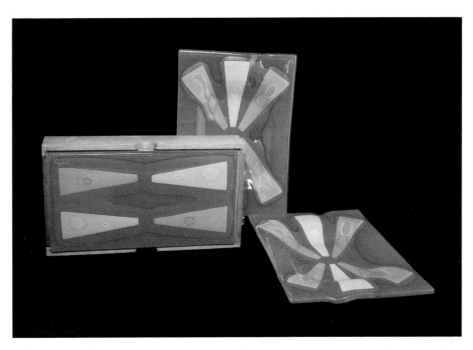

4.40 Smoking set of two rectangular ashtrays and wooden box with cover in same pattern of bright orange with orange and white triangles. 7" length of ashtray, 7 1/2" box top. 40-60 each; 90-100

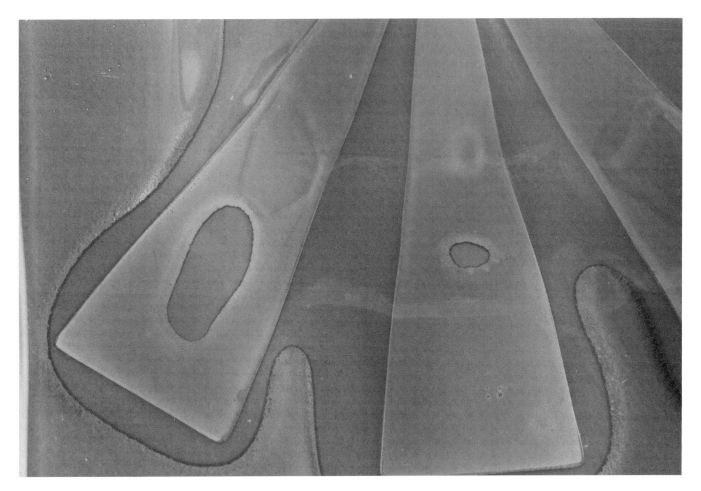

4.41 Detail of triangle. ·

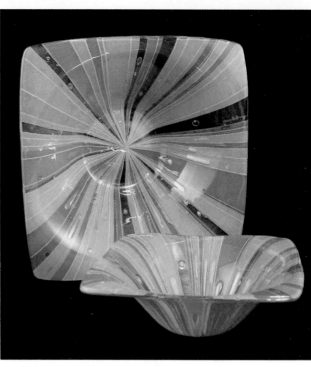

4.42 Bowls with yellow and blue stripes radiating from the center, with etched signature between layers of glass, 7 1/4" square and 5 1/4" square. *Courtesy of Donna and Rodney Wasserstrom.* 75-100; 50-60

4.44 Bowls with orange stripes radiating from the center, 10" square and 7 1/8" square, with etched signatures between layers of glass. *Courtesy of Donna and Rodney Wasserstrom.* 100-125; 75-100

4.43 Detail of stripes and air bubbles.

4.45 Detail of stripes.

4.46 Freeform plate with green, yellow, and orange butterflies. 9 5/8" longest side, with Dearborn signature. *Courtesy of Studio Moderne.* 85-105

4.47 Detail of butterflies.

4.48 Freeform plate with birds in orange, yellow, and blue. 9 5/8" longest side, with Dearborn signature. 85-105

4.49 Detail of birds.

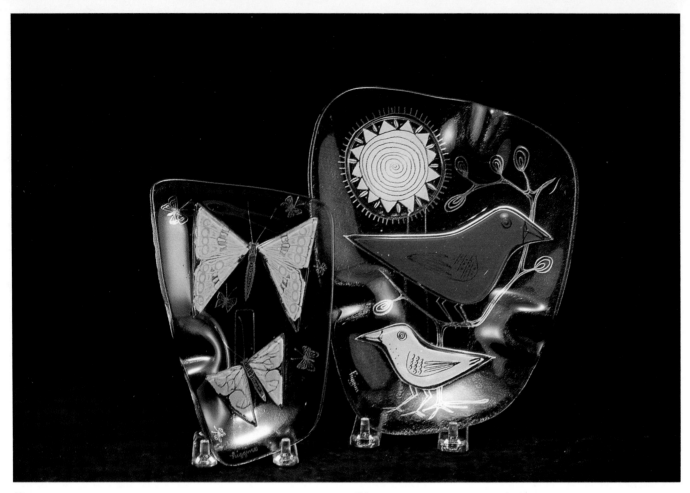

Above:
4.50 Left, freeform plate with colorful butterflies, 9"; right, freeform ashtray with red and white birds, 7" length, with Dearborn signatures. 85-105 each

Below:
4.51 Round ashtrays with stripes radiating from the centers: top, orange and yellow, 6 1/2"; bottom, orange and yellow, 5 1/2"; right, orange and olive green, 6" diameter, Dearborn signatures. 35-45 each

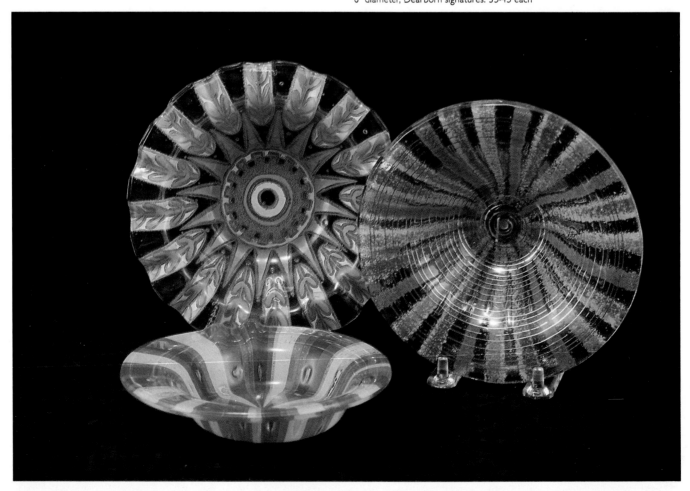

4.52 Multicolored chipped ice design on ashtray of irregular shape with pink center. with original paper sticker and Dearborn signature, 9 1/4" length. 125-150

4.53 Detail of chipped ice.

Below:
4.54 Detail of center.

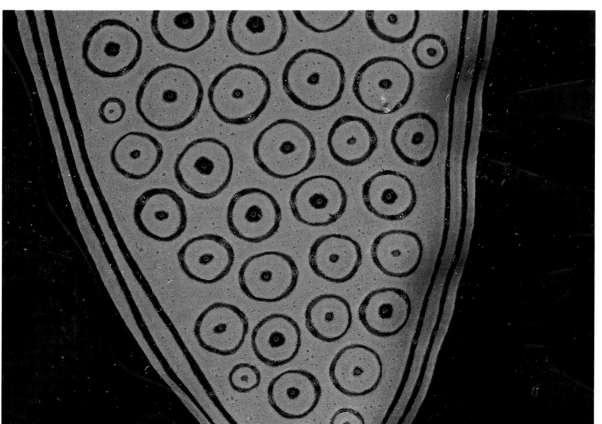

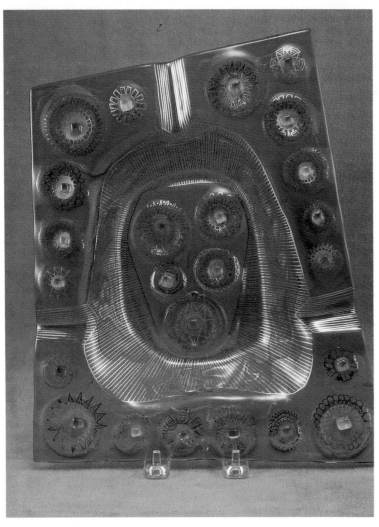

4.55 Jewels design with multicolored glass bits applied to the surface of ashtray in irregular shape, 12" length, Dearborn signature. 135-165

4.56 Detail of jewels.

4.57 Pocket watches on rectangular ashtrays: left 7 x 10"; center 9 3/4 x 14"; right, 5 x 7" length, Dearborn signatures. 100-125; 125-150; 75-95

4.58 Rectangular ashtray with blue and green fish, 10" length, Dearborn signature. 100-125

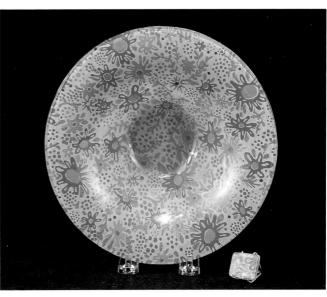

4.60 Bowl with small orange mums: bowl 8 1/4" with Dearborn signature; matching ring, 1". 100-125; 50-75

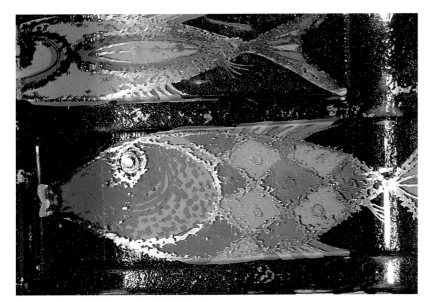

4.59 Detail of fish.

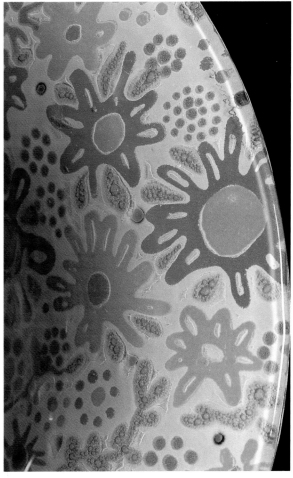

4.61 Detail of mums.

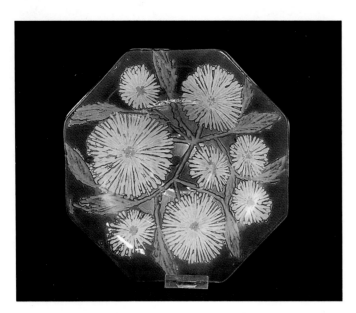

4.62 Yellow chrysanthemums on brown octagonal plate, 8 1/4", signed between glass layers. 100-120

4.63 Detail of chrysanthemums.

4.64 Yellow mums on octagonal bowl, 8 1/4", Dearborn signature. 115-135

4.65 Bowl with beige and brown flowers, 8", etched signature. 115-135

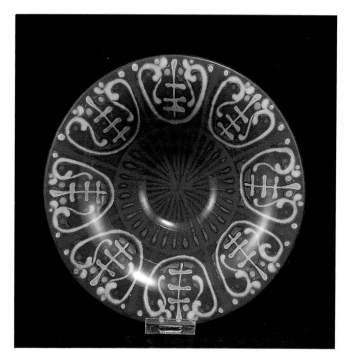

4.67 Red 8 1/2" bowl with Chinese calligraphy design and etched signature. 100-120

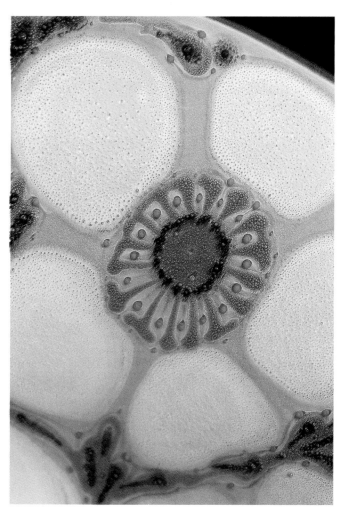

4.66 Detail of flowers.

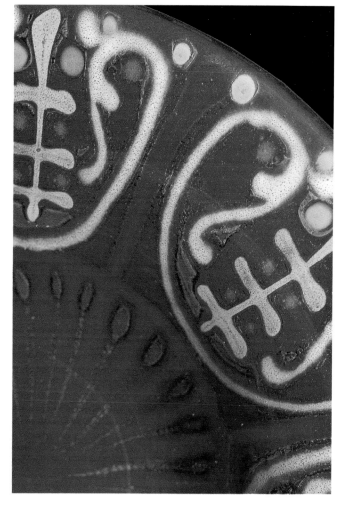

4.68 Detail.

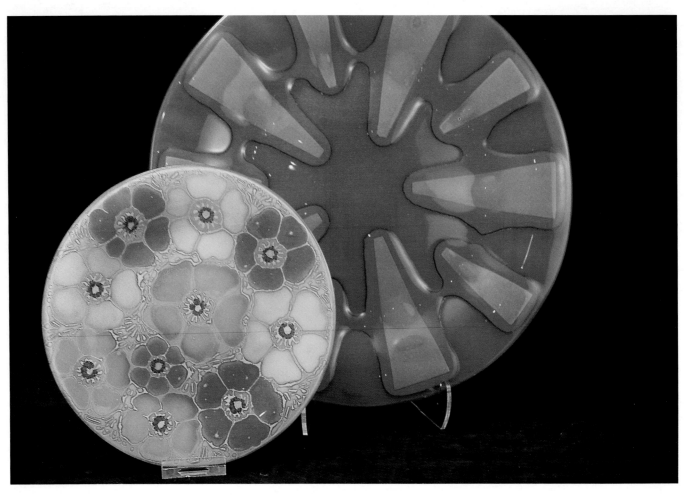

4.69 Left, plate with red and orange flowers, 7 1/2" with etched stickman signature; right, plate with red and orange spokes, 12 3/8". Dearborn signature. 125-150; 100-125

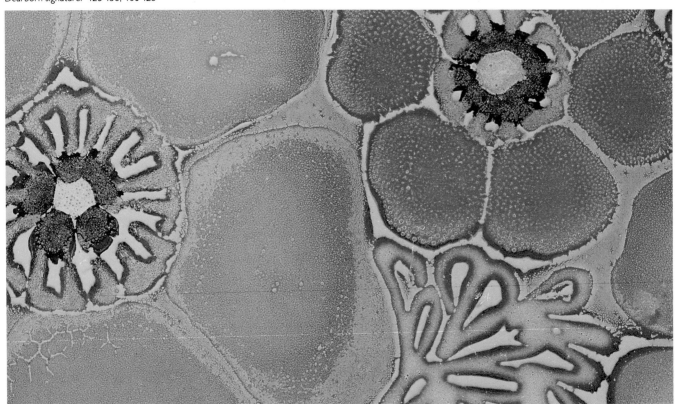

4.70 Detail of flowers.

4.71 Orange rectangular ashtrays with triangle decoration: left, 10" length; right, 7" length, Dearborn signatures. 70-80; 50-60

4.72 Bowl with red, orange, and periwinkle blue flowers, 12 3/4" diameter, with etched signature. 175-225

4.73 Stained glass design ashtray in orange, black, grey, and brown with original paper label, 7" length, Dearborn signature. 135-160

4.74 Detail of stained glass.

4.75 Detail of stained glass.

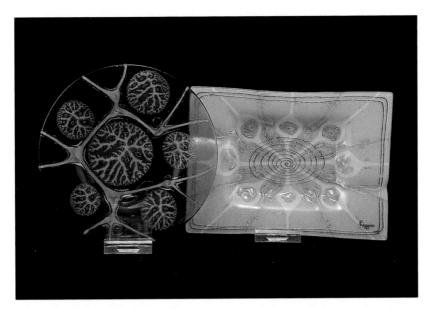

4.76 Left, pink puffballs on round 6" plate; right, white and green rectangular ashtray, 7" length, Dearborn signatures. 70-90; 50-60

4.77 Left, 5" square ashtray with daisies; right, three-compartment 9 1/2" round bowl with daisies, Dearborn signatures. 60-70; 135-155

4.78 Orange plate with black Oriental tree motif, 8 1/2" diameter, Dearborn signature. 85-110

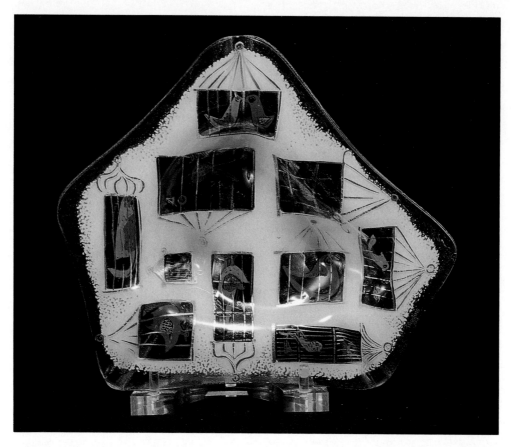

4.79 Yellow ashtray of irregular shape with birds inside square reserves, 9 1/2" across, Dearborn signature. 150-175

4.80 Detail of bird.

4.81 Blue bowl with yellow and red stripes radiating from the center and etched signature, 12 3/4" diameter. 175-225

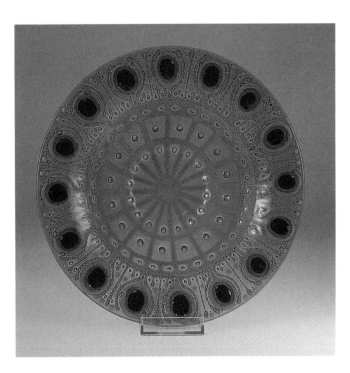

4.83 Bowl with blue wheel spoke pattern and peacock feather motif around the rim, 8 3/4" diameter, with etched signature. 100-125

4.82 Three-compartment bowl in blues, 13 1/2", Dearborn signature. 175-225

4.84 Fluted blue ashtray, 6 7/8" diameter, Dearborn signature. 55-65

4.85 Square 14" bowl with purple, blue, and yellow swirls, Dearborn signature. 225-275

4.86 Wood box with 7 x 7 3/4" glass cover and 7" matching ashtray with blue and purple abstract stripes resembling torn paper, Dearborn signatures. 90-110; 50-60

4.87 Bowl with abstract pattern in blue tones, 12 1/2" diameter. *Courtesy of Arthur and Ruth Marcus.* 150-175

4.88 Unusual soft blue vase with yellow striped base, satin finish, and etched signature, 4 1/2" height. 150-195

Chapter Five:
More Designers of Note

Gay Fad

One company that produced tumblers and bent glass items with gold screened decorations resembling those of Georges Briard was Gay Fad Studios of Lancaster, Ohio. These signed Briard look-alikes, however, were only a small portion of this company's glass product, which was usually decorated by hand and unsigned.

The founder and company head, Detroit artist Fran Taylor, began by decorating metal wastebaskets in her home. Immediate success enabled her to open a company to decorate a variety of kitchen items, such as canisters and trays. The decision to use glass for these hand painted decorations warranted that they move closer to a glassmaking area, and in 1945 Lancaster was the selected site. Among the companies to provide glass blanks were Federal, Hazel Atlas, Libbey, West Virginia Glass and Specialty Co., Zanesville, and Anchor Hocking with a plant across the road from Gay Fad Studios.

Decorations and forms were mostly traditional, although typical Fifties themes, such as tropical plants and animals, covered the tall thin tumblers (Zombies) and other items. Enamel colors were permanently fused to the glass by gradually bringing it up to a firing temperature and then cooling it just as slowly. This production, which was the company's mainstay, began in 1946.

Decorations and product types were changed twice a year, a practice common to seasonal industries. At one time there were approximately 400 different items in the line. By the 1950s a silk screening method was introduced in order to meet production demand; some patterns were partly screened and partly painted by hand. These technologies enabled another 500 design patterns to be added in the mid 1950s. The screened abstract and other modern designs on bent glass were introduced late. But foreign competition, financial difficulties, and personal problems had already taken their toll. Taylor sold the plant in 1963, and the company closed two years later.

5.1 Long rectangular three-pocket server decorated with gold leaves, signed GAY FAD, 8 x 22". 20-30

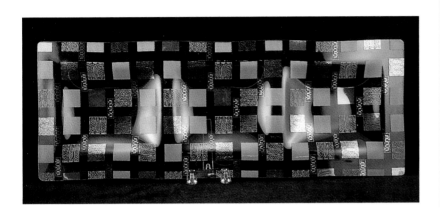

5.2 Long rectangular three-pocket server in turquoise checkerboard design, signed GAY FAD, 8 x 22". 25-35

5.3 Detail with signature.

5.4 Long rectangular tray with white abstract design on clear glass, signed GAY FAD, 8 x 22". 25-35

Thelma Frazier Winter

Thelma Frazier (1903-1977) began her art career as a student at the Cleveland School of Art, an institution that served as a center for the development of a "Cleveland School" of painting and decorative arts. She later taught there, as well as in Cleveland public schools, and influenced many other artists, especially in the field of ceramics.

From 1928 until the company closed in 1930, Thelma worked for the Cowan Pottery Co., just a few miles from the art school in the suburb of Rocky River, Ohio. There she made limited edition vases and plaques, crackle glazed plates, and pieces with relief designs and opalescent glazes. Throughout her long career, clay sculpture interested her most, and it can be easily recognized by its humor and whimsy.

In 1939 she married Edward Winter. After Winter traveled to Vienna with ceramic artists Viktor Schreckengost and Russel Aitken to study at the Kunstgewerbeschule (arts and crafts school) in Vienna, he contributed to bringing the Viennese style of ceramic design to Cleveland. This style became one of the most noticeable influences on Thelma's work.

The Cleveland May Show, the annual juried exhibit held at the Cleveland Museum of Art, was another important focus of the Cleveland art scene, and Thelma Frazier Winter exhibited and won prizes at the shows in the 1930s and 1940s. In 1939 she was the first woman to win a prize in ceramic sculpture at another very prestigious exhibit, the Ceramic National in Syracuse, New York. Although ceramic art was her mainstay, she also produced whimsical enameled copper pieces with the signature "Thelma" on the front and "Winter" on the back.

5.5 Rectangular pocket server with white abstract design on clear glass, signed GAY FAD, 15 3/4 x 9 3/4". 30-40

5.6 Enamel on copper plate with butterfly motif, signed THELMA on the front and WINTER on the back, 7 1/8" diameter. 50-60

5.7 Enamel on copper plate with girl and cat motif, signed THELMA on the front and WINTER on the back, 11 1/4" diameter. 70-90

5.9 Enamel on copper plate with pink-winged angel, signed THELMA on the front and WINTER on the back, 11 1/2" diameter. 70-90

5.8 Enamel on copper ashtray with deep turquoise rim and same girl and cat, 11" diameter. 70-90

5.10 Enamel on copper plate with mice motif, signed THELMA on the front and WINTER on the back, 11" diameter. 70-90

5.11 Enamel of copper abstract still life with fruit and wine glass, signed THELMA, 11"
diameter. 250-350

5.12 Detail.

5.13 Detail.

Nekrassoff

Serge Nekrassoff (1893-1985) was born in Russia and left after the Revolution. While apprenticing in a Parisian metalworking shop, he developed a method of hammering copper that enabled him to shape the metal without the usual annealing process. When he could afford to pay for a steamship ticket and a month's rent, he sailed to Buenos Aires, Argentina and opened his first shop.

In the 1920s Argentine taste was similar to the French, and he continued to produce elaborately ornamented pieces. His talent and popularity brought him the financial success needed to go to the United States, and he sailed to New York and opened a shop in 1925. However, the ornate designs did not sell, and he adapted to the current taste for simpler and more modern forms.

By the late 1920s Nekrassoff was painting with fine powdered glass on copper; in fact, he was one of the few artists to work with enamels at that time. After shaping a flat copper disc into a plate, it was sprayed with glue. A thin layer of colored ground glass (enamel powder) was added, and the piece was fired in a kiln. After cooling, the piece was painted with goldfinches, cedar waxwings, cardinals, scarlet tanagers, chickadees, quail, pelicans, bald eagles, gulls, robins, and other birds. Many of these pieces, produced for several decades, were sold through Abercrombie and Fitch Co.

In 1931, Nekrassoff moved to Darien, Connecticut, where he worked in pewter, copper, and enamel on copper. His son Boris joined him to design and make decorative items and to supervise the work of up to eighteen craftsmen. Each piece was stamped with the work "Nekrassoff" in the metal on the bottom. Enameled bird pieces were also signed on the front. After World War II copper became the main metal used, and seven master craftsmen formed their staff. From 1952 to 1979 father and son operated the shop called "Serge S. Nekrassoff and Son" in Stuart, Florida.

5.16 Enamel on copper shallow bowl with robin feeding its young, signed NEKRASSOFF, 9" diameter. 80-100

5.14 Enamel on copper shallow bowl with seagulls over the water, signed NEKRASSOFF, 9" diameter. 80-100

5.15 Detail of gulls.

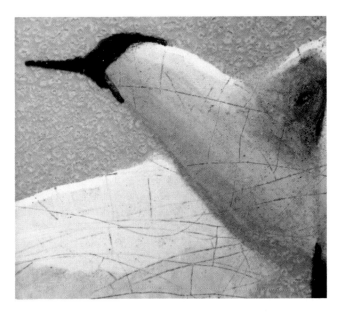

5.17 Detail of robins.

Couroc

Couroc® is a name associated with a unique item—a black plastic tray or box with hand inlaid decoration. The company also produced a line of decorated and signed glassware. In 1948 a man by the name of Guthrie Courvoisier, an industrialist, owner of a San Francisco art gallery, and descendant of the renowned French brandy family, founded the company in Monterey, California. Courvoisier had worked with plastics and resins while in the military. After the war he developed a method of inlaying natural materials, such as woods and metals, into a compound called phenolic resin. The first letters of his name "COU" + "ROC" for the rock hard material formed the company name Couroc.

The unlikely combination of plastic and handcrafted inlay produced a remarkable item. Not normally signed on the front, one

5.19 Detail of owl.

5.18 Owl motif on glasses, signed COUROC. 4-7 each

design, Monterey Cypress by S. F. B. Morse, does have an inlaid signature. (Georges Briard was invited to design for them, but didn't get around to it.) Courac is currently producing new patterns of the inlaid plastic along with a few of the classics from the 1950s and 1960s such as Monterey Cypress. Although the signed glassware is from the 1960s and has not been produced for many years, a new line of barware is currently being introduced. These will feature some of the classic tray patterns that have not yet been used for glassware.

5.20 Mushroom design on glasses, signed COUROC. 4-7 each

5.21 Kachina design on glasses, signed COUROC, in front of matching tray, both from the 1960s. 4-7 each; 40-50

5.22 Although Couroc black plastic trays are not usually signed by the designer or on the front, this example, called Monterey Cypress and dated 1966, has the designer signature S. F. B. MORSE inlaid along with the design. 100-125

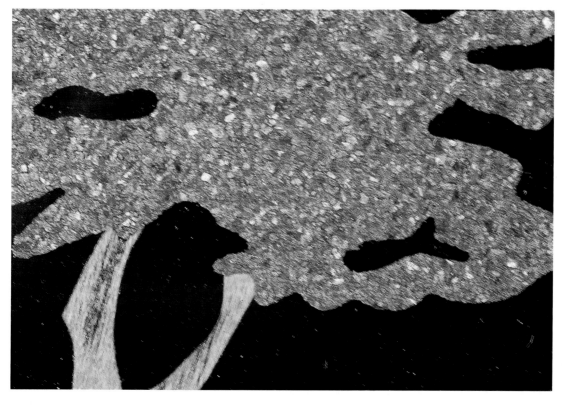

5.23 Detail of tree.

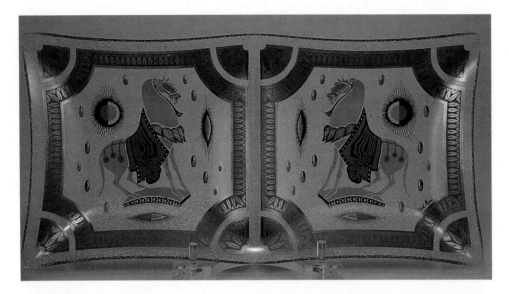

Fred Press
and other designers

5.24 Two part server with blue horse motif, signed FRED PRESS, 6 3/4 x 13 1/2". 15-25

5.25 Detail of horse.

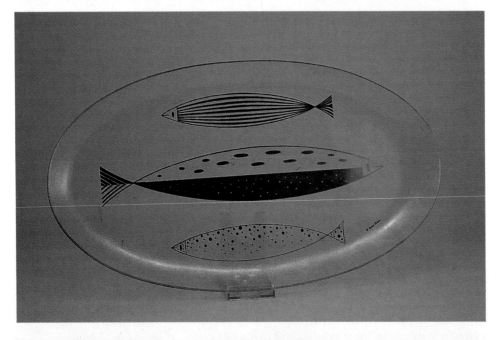

5.26 Oval platter in textured glass like Briard's aura and gold motif of three fish, signed FRED PRESS, 16 5/8 x 9 1/4". 12-18

5.27 Black horse motif on square plate, signed FRED PRESS, 11 3/4". 15-25

5.29 Plain gold striped pocket server, signed LEE HAGER, 13 1/2" square. 15-20

5.28 Square 5 3/4" plate in textured glass like Briard's aura, signed ROJAC. *Courtesy of Ade and Marv Eppell.* 6-8

5.30 Roly poly glass with version of Briard's Forbidden Fruit pattern in gold, signed CULVER LTD. Culver had been known for their more traditional designs on glassware until they collaborated with Georges Briard to produce his gold screened patterns. They then went on to produce other contemporary designs with the Culver label. 3-5

5.31 Suburban glasses in stained glass motif, signed NED HARRIS. 7-9 each

5.32 Opaque white glass plate with copy of Briard's Forbidden Fruit pattern, signed GABOR, 7 3/4" square. 8-10

5.33 Other Briard look-alikes: left, tumblers with liquor bottle design, signed BOB WALLACK; right small glasses with horse and chariot, signed FRED PRESS. 3-5 each

Signatures

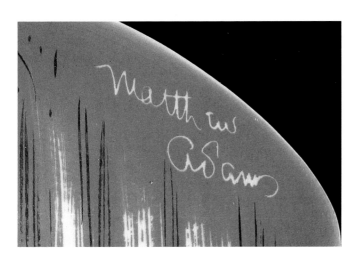

Matthew Adams (front)

Matthew Adams (back/base)

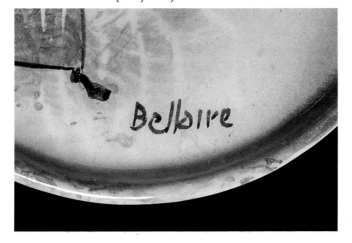

Bellaire (front)

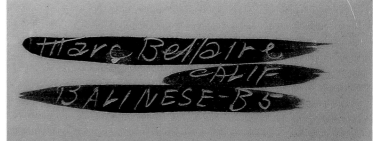

Marc Bellaire Balinese (back/base)

Marc Bellaire Friendly Island (back/base)

Marc Bellaire Mardi Gras (back/base)

Sascha B. (Front)

Georges Briard in gold

Sascha Brastoff California USA (rooster backstamp on back/ base) with handwritten model number D2

Georges Briard in black

Georges Briard with ©

Georges Briard Glass Guild

Couroc ©

Gay Fad

Gay Fad

Gabor

214

Higgins (gold Dearborn signature on front)

Nekrassoff

Fred Press

Bob Wallack

Appendix A
Georges Briard Patterns

Alhambra

1957-1967 catalogs

Major patterns used on a variety of items and/or especially popular designs in **bold**

Alhambra

Ambrosia (Pineapple)

Arabesque

Arbor

Art Gallery

Art Nouveau

Athenia

Balloon

Bar Manners

Baroco

Batik

Bar Manners

Ambrosia

Athenia

Batik

Baroco

Bijoux

Bee

Bijoux

Birdcage

Blue Orchard

Bottle

Bounty

Bouquet

Burgundy

Butterfly

Camellia

Cameo

Capri

Caprice

Carousel

Carrara

Cathay

Celeste

Burgundy

Butterfly

Cameo

Capri

Carousel

Cathay

Celeste

Charleston Gardens

Cheers

Colonial

Coq Rouge

Credit Card

Delft

Chanticleer

Charleston Garden

Cheers

Chess

Dove

Classique

Colonial

Coq D'or

Coq Rouge

Cornucopia

Coronet

Credit Card

Delft

Dinner at 8

Domino

Dove

Duchess

East Wind

Eldorado

Embassy

Empire

Enchanted Forest

Europa

Eye Ball

Duchess

Eldorado

Embassy

Europa

Eye Ball

Facade

Fancy Free

Federal

Facade

Fancy Free

Federal

Fleurette

Fleur Noir

Floral Jungle

Floriana

Florentine

Fontainebleau

Forbidden Fruit

Frieze

Fruit Frolic

Galaxy

Garden of Eden

Golden Harvest

Gold Link

Granada

Green Garden

Floral Jungle

Floriana

Florentine

Forbidden Fruit

Fruit Frolic

Galaxy

Garden of Eden

Golden Harvest

Granada

Green Garden

Hapsburg

Hapsburg

Hawaii

Health Bar

Heaven Can Wait

Heritance

Hexometric

Iberia

Ice Gold

Imperial Garden

International Time

Janus

King High

Lady in the Rain

La Scala

Lemon

Lemon Tree

Lido

Linometric

Hawaii

Health Bar

Heritance

Iberia

Imperial Garden

International Time

Janus

King High

Lemon Tree

Linometric

Lido

Mandarin

Marlborough

Matador

Moonglow

Muddled Wisdom

Lotus

Lucky Eight

Lute Song

Lyric

Mandarin

Marblesque

Marlborough

Matador

Mediterranean

Melange

Melon

Moonglow

Muddled Wisdom

Music

Name Your Poison

Nautica

Old Orchard

Olympia

Onion

Op Box

Op Wave

Painted Daisy

Palais Royal

Palazzo

Name your Poison

Old Orchard

Olympia

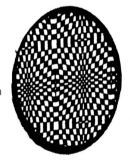

Op Box

Op Wave

Palais Royal

Paradise

Patio Rose

Patterns

Persia

Persian Garden

Regalia

Pickled Personality

Plaisirs D'Amour

Primavera

Province

Regalia

Regency

Rex

Rondo

Roman Holiday

Rose Blush

Royal Club

Royal Crest

Paradise

Rex

Patio Rose

Rondo

Patterns

Persian Garden

Roman Holiday

Plaisirs D'Amour

Pickled Personality

Royal Crest

Royal Club

Samoa

Samoa

Sampler

Santilla

Sari

Scintilla

Scotch

Seascape

Ship

Ship Ahoy

Silver Damask

Silver Loom

Sonata

Sorrento

Spanish Coin

Spanish Gold

Spiral

Stellar

Still Life

Strawberry

Sunburst

Sunflower

Sampler

Sari

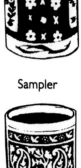

Scotch

Seascape

Ship Ahoy

Silver Damask

Sonata

Sorrento

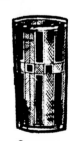

Sunburst

Spanish Gold

Stellar

Surf

Sutton Place

Taj Mahal

Tempo

Thirst Extinguisher

Tiara

Surf

Sutton Place

Taj Mahal

Tapestry

Tempo

Thirst Extinguisher

Tiara

Tiffany

Tortoise

Town & Country

Trifle

Tropicana

Tulip Tree

Versailles

Victorian Trifle

Vignette

Vineland

Vintage

Wall Street

Wayside Inn

Wet Your Whistle

Wisteria

Tiffany

Tropicana

Tulip Tree

Versailles

Wall Street

Wayside Inn

Wet Your Whistle

Wisteria

Vintage

1970s barware

Anchors	Madrid
Anemone	Marac
Art Deco	Marshweed
	Metric
Balloons	Military Wedding
Bamboo	Moonflower
Band	Mouse
Bird	
Brando	Nautical
Cabana	Pansy
Cane	Peacock
Captain	Polka Poppy
Chain	
Chromatic	Rally
Cold	
	Santa
Decoy	Sentinal
	Shell
Feather Bouquet	Ski
Fern	Smoke Ice
Field Flower	Stainglass
Firenze	Stitched Leather
Fish	Straw
Frost Flower	Strawflower
	Stripes
Geese	Study in Brown
Golden Garden	
Goldnet	Teardrop
Gold Wire	Tennis
Golf	Tigerlily
Greenfield Hill	Town
Gull	Tree of Life
	Tulip
Harlequin	
	Weave
Icicle	Wildlife
Independence	Windows
	Wire Ice
Jungle	
	Zinnia
Kudo	
Ladybug	

Appendix B
Companies Producing Briard Designs

Georges Briard, under the name Georges Briard Designs, designed and distributed his products, while several different companies either licensed the designs or manufactured them for Briard. One company, M. Wille Inc., distributed several lines in the 1950s. When Georges Briard Designs formed a partnership with M. Wille they became known as M. Wille Inc. Georges Briard Designs (also Georges Briard M. Wille Inc.), which enhanced Briard's ability to control product design, assembly of some items, and distribution. If still in business, names and/or addresses of the following companies may have changed.

M. Wille Inc. Georges Briard Designs
225 Fifth Ave.
New York, NY 10010
Distribution and some assembly of Hostess accessories of brass and glass with tile, Barware, Porcelainite - porcelain enamel on steel with brass-plated stands, Toleware, and other Briard products

Allied Chemical - Plastics Division
40 Rector St.
New York, NY
Artisan Melamine dinnerware

Arden Furniture Co.
Brooklyn, NY
Eastwood hospitality carts; Railite synthetic wood-grain, stain and heat resistant

Art Gift Products Co.
Philadelphia, PA
Americana motif on metal accessories

Automatic Controls Corp.
Ann Arbor, MI
Kingsware electrified accessories of brass, walnut, and ceramic

Beach Products Inc.
One Paper Place
Kalamazoo, MI 49001
Contempo paperware, first licensee of Georges Briard lines

Columbian
Terre Haute IN
Color-way porcelain enamel cookware

Culver Glassware
1905 Elizabeth Ave.
Rahway NJ 07065
Glassware

English Silver Mfg. Corp.
Brooklyn NY
Eldorado buffet accessories - solid brass and copper

Fresco Co.
Bronx NY
Melamite shelves, occasional furniture of brass and walnut or ebony

Glass Guild
126-02 Metropolitan Ave.
Jamaica 15, NY
Flat formed glass (White Opal, Aura, Gold, Mandarin Orange, or Peacock Blue) with hand-applied 22-karat gold; mosaic art – ceramic inlaid on brass-finished anodized aluminum with glass insert and colored glass mosaic

Goldcrest Inc.
Mt. Vernon NY
Solid brass hostess accessories

Hartman Associates
Long Island NY
Imported fine china and serving accessories, Très Briard ceramic ashtrays

Hyalyn Porcelain
Hickory NC
Briard shapes and decoration of bisque porcelain, some used as lamp bases for Lightolier

J & H International Corp.
7400 Caldwell Ave.
Chicago IL 60648
Dinnerware and home accessories.

Lightolier
100 Lighting Way
Secaucus NJ 07094
Lamps using Hyalyn porcelain bases designed by Briard

Mdina Glass
Malta
Art glass imported and distributed by Georges Briard

N. F. C. Engineering Co.
Anoka MN
Pola-therm insulated servers

Peerless Art Co.
Brooklyn NY
Pola-therm insulated barware, sculptured gold glassware

Pfaltzgraff Pottery
140 East Market St.
York NY 17401
Heritage pattern

Shayne Products Co.
2255 N. Ninth St.
Philadelphia PA 19133
Lava wood ice buckets

Solarserve
Brooklyn NY
Acrylic with tile inserts

Stetson Products (see Allied Chemical)

H. J. Stotter Inc.
New York NY
Carefree table-top fashions: place mats, bar mats, coasters

Woodland Co.
Glen Falls NY
Walnut cheese boards with tile inserts, mahogany, and other wood servers

Select Bibliography

Anderson, Harriette. *Kiln-fired Glass.* Philadelphia: Chilton Book Co., 1970.

Anderson, Ross and Barbara Perry. *The Diversions of Keramos: American Clay Sculpture 1925-1950.* Syracuse: Everson Museum of Art, 1983.

Anderson, Winslow. Personal interview, Milton, West Virginia, Dec. 1993.

Barnes, Dwight. "A touch of glass." *Lancaster Eagle-Gazette* (Jan. 11, 1995): C-1.

_____. "More than a passing Fad." *Lancaster Eagle-Gazette* (Jan. 4, 1995): A-8.

"Bellaire, Marc." in *Who's Who in California 16, 1986-87.*

Bellaire, Marc. *Brush Decoration.* Columbus, Ohio: Professional Publications, 1957.

_____. *Underglaze Decoration.* Columbus, Ohio: Professional Publications, 1964.

_____. Promotional material from Bellaire Studio, 1980s.

Brastoff, Sascha. "Sculpture in Steel: Sascha Brastoff." exhibit brochure. Los Angeles, 1955.

Brojdo, Jascha (Georges Briard). Personal interviews and telephone interviews 1994 and 1995.

Chipman, Jack. *Collector's Encyclopedia of California Pottery.* Paducah, Kentucky: Collector Books, 1992.

Cleveland Museum of Art. "Sascha Brastoff" in Artist Files, folder of clippings from periodicals such as *The Cleveland Plain Dealer, Cleveland Press, New Yorker Magazine,* etc.

Conti, Steve et al. *Collector's Encyclopedia of Sascha Brastoff.* Paducah, Kentucky: Collector Books, 1995.

Cox, Susan. "Sascha Brastoff, Innovator for All Times." *American Clay Exchange* (Nov. 1983).

"Designer Spotlight: Georges Briard." *China, Glass & Tableware* (Nov. 1983): 8.

Fifty-50. "Fused Glass: The Artisanry of Frances and Michael Higgins." exhibit catalog. New York: Fifty-50, 1986.

"Gay Fad Studios Aggressive, Growing Industry." *Lancaster Eagle-Gazette* (June 3, 1950).

Georges Briard Designs. Company catalogs, price lists, photographs, and other records from the 1950s through the 1980s.

_____. Dinnerware Products Publicity. Collection of clippings Dec. 1965 through Oct. 1966.

"Georges Briard Paints Profit Into Plastics." *Housewares Buyer* (Oct. 1966): 48.

Grover, Ray and Lee. *Contemporary Art Glass.* New York: Crown, 1975.

Higgins, Frances. Telephone interview, Jan. 1995.

Junius, H. D. E. "Present Popularity of Hand Wrought Hammered Pewter." *The Jewelers Circular - Keystone* (Feb. 1935):77.

Kovel, Ralph and Terry. "Nekrassoff." *Kovels on Antiques and Collectibles Newsletter.* (March 1987).

"Master Coppersmith." *Science Illustrated* (Jan. 1949).

McGrady, Donna. "Gay Fad Studios blossomed in postwar era." *Antique Week Central Edition* 24 (Dec. 9, 1991):1 & 36.

"Nekrassoff's Craftsmanship Featured in Magazine Story." *Darien (Connecticut)Review* (Jan. 6, 1949).

"Nekrassoffs Produce Attractive Gifts in Plant on U. S. 1 Here." unknown Florida newspaper (1950).

Piña, Leslie. "Sascha Brastoff" in *Pottery: Modern Wares 1920-1960.* Atglen, Pennsylvania: Schiffer, 1994.

Polak, Ada. "Signatures on Gallé Glass." *Journal of Glass Studies 8* (1966): 120-123.

Reese, Annie. "High Style, Fashion Treatment Brighten '66 Dinnerware Scene." *National Jeweler* (Jan. 1966).

Saunders, Carole. "What makes a top designer?" *Gift & Tableware Reporter* (Nov. 7, 1966).

"Serge Nekrassoff, Artist in Ceramics and Metals, Has Studio Here." *The Stuart* (Florida) *News* (May 4, 1969): 7-C.

Stetson, Philip. Partner in Georges Briard Designs, personal and telephone interviews 1994 and 1995.

Index

Gabor, 210; signature, 213
Galaxy pattern, 90
Gallé, Emile, 5
Gay Fad Studios, 200-202; signature, 213
Georges Briard (see Briard, Georges)
Georges Briard Designs, 5, 14-20; patterns, 215-219; companies producing, 220
Glass Guild, 14, 15, 17
Gold Damask pattern, 54
Golden Celeste pattern, 59-60
Golden Harvest pattern, 48-49
Golf Pattern, 100
Green Garden pattern, 38, 40-41
Gustavsberg Pottery, 15

Haeger Pottery, 117, 170
Hager, Lee, 209
Harris, Ned, 210
Hauser, John W., 17
Hazel Atlas Glass Co., 200
Heaven Can Wait pattern, 13, 77
Heritage pattern, 16
Heritance pattern, 61
Higgins Glass, 170; signature, 214
Higgins, Frances, 170
Higgins, Michael, 170
Holiday Greetings pattern, 126
Houze Glass, 5
Huttner, Esta, 15, 16
Hyalyn Porcelain, 15-16, 68-74

Iberia pattern, 24, 58
Imperial Garden pattern, 57
Imperial Malachite pattern, 108

Jamaica pattern, 154-55
Jewel Bird pattern, 125
J & H International, 115
Jungle Dancer pattern, 167

Kage, Wilhelm, 15
Kahnweiler, David, 12
Kashmir pattern, 163
Kourishima, Eddie, 117

Lazarus department store, 19
Lee Hager (see Hager, Lee)
Lemon Tree pattern, 23
Libbey Glass Co., 15, 200
Lightolier Lamp Co., 15, 74
Linometric pattern, 75
Luau pattern, 165

Madawick, Tucker P., 17
Mardi Gras pattern, 151-54
Marina Metal Arts Co., 117
Max, Peter, 5, 6
Melange pattern, 35-36, 99
Memphasis pattern, 17, 109
Merle Norman Cosmetics, 117
Misty Blue pattern, 133
Modern Geometry tables, 98
Morse, S. F. B., 206, 207
Mosaic line, 80-83

National Housewares Manufacturers Association (NHMA), 17
Ned Harris (see Harris, Ned)
Nekrassoff, Boris, 205
Nekrassoff, Serge, 205; signature, 214

L'Oignon ironstone, 34
Olympia pattern, 58
Op Art pattern, 27, 95
Orange Pageant pattern, 67
Oriental pattern, 166
Oriental Peacock pattern, 108

224